Horsefeathers
The Therapeutic Effect of Equus

Lillian Tepera

Horsefeathers
The Therapeutic Effect of Equus

Lillian Tepera

Outskirts Press, Inc.
Denver, Colorado

Outskirts Press, Inc.
http://www.outskirtspress.com

ISBN: 978-1-4327-5403-7

Outskirts Press and the "OP" logo are trademarks belonging to Outskirts Press, Inc.

PRINTED IN THE UNITED STATES OF AMERICA

Acknowledgments

I am deeply grateful to my editor, Kathryn Dean, and to my readers, Coralee Young and Joanne Kaplinski; this book could not have come together without your help and guidance.

I would also like to thank our Stonegate Farm volunteers, riders and their families for serving as my inspiration, not just in writing, but also in life. Although your names have been changed and your identities disguised, you know who you are and what you mean to me.

To the many horses in my life, a humble "thank you" for the joy you bring.

To my late uncle Voloda, thank you for having a passion for horses as great as mine, and to the rest of my family, know that I appreciate your traveling this road with me.

Table of Contents

Prologue

Walking into Krystal's grandma's house, I felt as if I was stepping over a time threshold, to days when I was a teenager myself, a horse-crazy kid with little opportunity to indulge that passion. When my family moved to Canada from what was then Czechoslovakia, we left everything we owned behind. My parents walked off the DC9 at Pearson Airport in Toronto with $20 in their pockets and only a vague idea of what to expect from this new country. We spent many years without much money. But in a number of the places where we lived in the early days, I had friends who had even less. In a little town where we spent two years while my father was away helping build the Churchill Falls generating station in Labrador, several of my friends lived in the local trailer park, so Krystal's grandma's modest little trailer was not completely strange to me. Now I was being escorted to the kitchen table by Grandma Edna, a tiny woman whose energy and courage would come to amaze me.

As we walked past the fridge, I was struck by the sight of two pictures that had been taped to it. They were pictures of my horse, Oscar, whom Krystal had been riding for eight weeks now at my farm. It shouldn't have surprised me to see him there. Lots of riders took pictures of the horses they rode in our program for special-needs children. But I realized, seeing Oscar's elegant head, with its narrow blaze, long ears and dark eyes staring at me from Edna's fridge, that I hadn't fully understood the impact of my horses on the lives of the people who rode them. Their realities and the way my horses had become part of them, had remained theoretical until this moment at Edna's kitchen table.

As a kid I'd had horse pictures all over my house, too, though mine were mostly drawings copied from books I'd borrowed from the library. Real horses were much harder for me to come by. My sister had gone out for a while with a boy from school whose family raised ponies, and I'd wheedled an invitation once or twice, but the ponies were used for driving competitions, not for riding, so all I could do was pat their noses and feed them carrots. I thought I'd hit paydirt one day when my best friend, Michelle, announced unexpectedly that her parents had bought a horse. We rushed over after school to see him. I could hardly contain myself. He was a big-bodied Appaloosa with loud markings, one blue eye, and a short, stiff mane that stuck straight up from his cresty neck. I was smitten. Visions of carefree gallops through the countryside played like a TV movie in my mind, complete with orchestral music.

Unfortunately, he turned out to be too wild for us to ride – or anyone else, for that matter. For years he lived in a small paddock behind Michelle's parents' house, more a lawn-ornament than a working horse, weirdly out of place among the ordinary back-yards surrounding him with their swingsets and kiddie pools. Watching him over the fence would be as close as Michelle and I would come to Horse. He and his cool name held me in awe, but he was strictly off-limits.

So it would be years before I could decorate my wall or fridge with pictures of real live horses that I was actually able to ride. They added a touch of reality in amongst the sketches of magnificent Lipizzan stallions from the Spanish Riding School and nameless Arabians, Quarter Horses, Palominos and Morgans copied from the stacks of library books I brought home every week.

On this cold and rainy autumn day I'd been invited to a meeting of Krystal's support team, all of whom were already seated at Edna's kitchen table when I arrived. I'd become an unofficial team member through my therapeutic riding program, and I'd been invited to the meeting today so I could explain an idea I'd proposed to one of Krystal's support workers. Edna had seen me glance at the photos on the fridge, and she laughed as I sat down.

"That's all Krystal talks about these days," she said in her surprisingly youthful voice. "Oscar this and Oscar that. If you let her bring him home, I'm sure he'd be sleeping in her bedroom."

The discussion started with a review of minutes from the previous month's meeting, which I had not attended. One note in the minutes was a comment from Edna about how Krystal had finally decided to get serious about school that fall. She would be headed to high school next year, and had announced to her family that it was time to start studying so she would do well.

"Do you know why?" Edna asked the group in general, then went on without waiting for an answer. "Because she wants a horse of her own some day. I support that. I had horses when I was young, too. But I told her, you won't afford a horse serving tea at the restaurant down the road. I don't know what it costs to keep a horse these days, but I know it costs plenty."

The meeting covered all the issues that were impacting this troubled family: from the problems Krystal and her siblings – all under Grandma Edna's care – were having at school, to Edna's need for a respite worker to come an extra few hours one day to look after her ailing husband so she could check out nursing homes for him, since the time would come when she could no longer care for him at home. While I found the list of issues overwhelming, Edna remained unfailingly optimistic. They would make it, she said. No matter what.

When it came my turn to explain what I was doing there, my idea seemed hopelessly insignificant.

"As you know," I said, "Krystal's sponsored lessons are finished now. The session she'd received funding for is over. But she mentioned to me more than once that she'd like to work with horses someday. So I thought of offering her a way to start. She could come to my farm on Saturday mornings and help out with the chores. Nothing glamorous. Scrubbing water buckets and sweeping cobwebs. Cleaning saddles. That kind of thing. Eventually, as she gets more experience, she could help groom the young horses I'm training and get them ready for work. In return for three hours' work, I'll give her a one-hour riding lesson. And the experience she gets might help her find a job on a farm one day."

"It's a dream come true for Krystal," Edna surprised me by saying, and the others nodded in agreement. "She wants to be with horses more than anything."

I watched the group talk excitedly about my proposal, and found that my nagging worries about feed bills and mortgage payments magically moved down the list of things to think about. So did the ever-present need to find more volunteers for the program, and the fact that I was exhausted from doing barn chores and schooling two horses that morning and still had my sons' football game to go to and a lesson to teach that night.

Maybe if I'd known right from the start exactly what I was getting myself into, I might have dismissed the idea of starting a therapeutic riding program. The amount of work and money required to set up the farm and keep it running had turned out to be far more than I had expected, and here I was knee-deep in alligators (banks, insurance companies, contractors etc.) with no time to drain the swamp.

Yet when someone asks me how I'm doing these days, my standard answer is always along the lines of "fantastic!" And it's true. I talk to people, read about people, know people, who have virtually no joy in their lives. Days drag. Work is drudgery. Family means nothing but heartache. Their glory-days, if ever they had them, have been left far behind in high-school or college. There's little to look forward to. And while they may not have the worries that I have about monumental bills and a seemingly endless amount of work to do, they also don't have the joy of watching someone's eyes light up when they walk through the doors of my barn and see "their" horse waiting for them on lesson night. Sure, it would be nice if a fairy godmother popped out of the ether and made all the debts go away, finished all the uncompleted projects still waiting in the house and the barn and the garage, or blessed me with a self-cleaning stable. But I'll manage without her, too. And it doesn't take much deep thinking about my own family or the kids who come out to ride my horses – kids like Krystal – to realize that none of the unpleasant stuff really matters.

1

The wind of heaven is that which blows between a horse's ears. (Arabian Proverb)

I packed up my books and my laptop, slinging three heavy bags over my shoulder: computer, assignments to be marked, and the textbooks I would need for prepping next week's classes. When I'd left my job in the corporate world, I hadn't realized the academic life would require so much heavy lifting.

It was quite a switch for me, learning the routines of teaching Marketing rather than practicing it. But I liked the change of pace; liked the students and the opportunity to actually think about things for a change, instead of always being in a hurry to act, as the high-tech universe in which I'd spent the previous twenty years of my working life had often forced me to do. Leaving the pressure cooker of high-technology for a teaching gig at the local community college had been liberating. The relatively leisurely pace of teaching certainly had its attractions.

And then I ruined it all by buying a horse farm. Giving up our little 6-acre backyard with barn for a real farm, and everything that real "farming" entails.

But at the moment my mind was on other things. I had a horse show to get ready for. As I loaded my bags into my Beetle and wheeled out of the parking lot a little more quickly than I probably should have, I was making a check-list in my head of all that had to be done in the course of the next two hours: post the show schedule in the barn for parents and riders to refer to, set up the arena with the necessary poles, pylons and props needed for the various competitions and games, make sure the ribbons, certificates and t-shirts for the riders were laid out, bring in the horses and start grooming them. This last bit would take extra time today, since we would be braiding manes and tails and decorating them with ribbons in addition to the regular brushing and hoof-cleaning. And the horses would need to be extra-shiny today. Many pictures would be taken. Thankfully, Krystal would be along to help out early, and Meghan and Sarah, too. They would be coming straight from school to help get the horses ready and then work with riders as they normally did during lessons.

I also needed my list of horse show "classes" – those tasks each rider would have to accomplish to earn his or her ribbon, based on the list of goals we'd laid out weeks ago when the riders first joined us. Because this was no ordinary horse show. It was graduation day for the latest group of riders in my therapeutic riding program. Only two of these riders had been on a horse before joining our program -- one was in fact a very capable rider, able to control a horse quite nicely on her own, while the other had been riding with us for several months now, and progressed to trotting despite quite significant physical and cognitive limitations caused by Cerebral Palsy. The other six ranged from a young girl who would require frequent breaks during the hour as her ability to concentrate ran out, to the tall, gangly teen-aged boy who polished up his cowboy boots for every lesson and prided himself on the extra "homework" he did each week to learn more about horses than I had in fact assigned. The common thread among all eight riders – split into two groups of four for their weekly lessons and the horse show -- was that each had been diagnosed with some form of developmental delay or disability. These riders had been hand-picked and funded by a community support agency to experience an enriched version of our regular therapeutic riding program – one that would teach some horse-manship skills as well as riding, and give the students a specific set of goals to accomplish, which they would demonstrate today in our "show."

For Connie, the little girl with the short attention-span, the pro-gram had proved challenging. Besides a lack of tolerance for odours – a definite problem when you're in a stable, and quite common in children with Autism – she had a tendency to be-come anxious when separated from her parents, even by the half-door of the arena. She became frightened easily. For her, one of the biggest challenges would be the beginning of today's horse show, when she would be required to lead her horse into the arena and through an obstacle course of pylons before coming to the mounting block to get on the horse and ride. She was intimidated by the horse's size – much more noticeable from the ground than from his back – and his tendency to rub his muzzle on her arm. Although the volunteer who worked with Connie was never more than a step or two away, Connie's courage and perseverance were stretched to the limit by this exercise.

But pushing the envelope was what this particular program was all about. Unlike the riders in our regular lessons who simply came and rode and then went home, these students went home with homework every week. That meant homework for the parents, too, but they seemed happy to do it. In week one they'd learned the names of different grooming tools – hoof picks, curry combs, dandy brushes – and took home a sheet that showed the names and pictures in two columns that had to be matched up. Of course, not all the riders could read, so the parents had to work with them to get the homework done. When learning parts of the horse, the parents had to read the names of different conformation points and have the children point to them on a drawing of a horse. Knee. Hock. Elbow. Muzzle. Mane. The end result was parents who now knew much more about horses than they had banked on learning! The children rose to the occasion and proudly showed off completed homework assignments at the beginning of each week's lesson.

I hoped Connie would make it through the scariest parts at the start without too many problems. The rest of the "show" would be easy for her after that.

The barn door opened as I was musing about Connie while tying a ribbon around a braid I'd just completed and I could hear Meghan and Sarah chatting as they walked in. When they saw what I was doing, they practically squealed with excitement.

"Awesome!" Sarah said. "Can I braid Wilby's mane?"

"Of course," I answered. "And Meghan, you can do Oscar if you'd like. Krystal should be here any minute to start on Louis. We need to have all four of them gussied up before the riders arrive."

The girls rushed off to get the horses and start braiding. Both were teen-agers who took riding lessons at a nearby competition barn, but neither had her own horse. Volunteering in my program gave them extra "horse time," and I tried to make sure they always got the opportunity to ride before the evening's lessons. Polishing up the horses for our little show seemed to make them almost as happy as braiding for a show they would be competing in themselves.

As the rest of the volunteers trickled in by ones and twos, I noticed everyone seemed to have a little extra bounce in their step. The evening had a real sense of occasion to it – a feeling that only got stronger when I unpacked the shirts I'd had made up for the occasion: dark blue polo shirts with the Stonegate Farm name and logo embroidered on them. It was little enough to give these dedicated volunteers as thanks for their hard work every week, but they all seemed delighted as they changed into their new shirts and joined in the brushing, braiding and tacking-up of the horses. And then the first of the riders came in.

It was Lisa, a delicate fourteen-year-old who had fallen madly, passionately in love with horses and riding. Before the session was even half-way over she was already pestering her parents about coming back for more lessons. Her eyes opened wide as she saw the horses.

"They look beautiful!" she exclaimed, the sight of our dolled-up beasties stopping her in her tracks. Then she walked to Henk, "her" horse for the duration of the program, and took him in from nose to tail: the gleaming black coat, the long French braid coiling along the crest of his neck and finished with a white ribbon at the end, the bow in his long, thick tail. There were tears in her eyes as she wrapped her arms around his neck and hugged him. Henk stretched his neck around as far as the cross-ties holding him would allow, and playfully lipped the back of Lisa's shirt. A year or two earlier, the lips might have been followed by his teeth, but he had done a great deal of growing up, and understood now that biting humans – even if it was meant to be playful – was simply not acceptable.

Once the other riders arrived, each one was handed the reins and instructed to lead his or her horse into the arena. The parents and grandparents followed as far as the arena doors, cameras dangling from straps around their necks. Each horse/rider combination was surrounded by its own little team of volunteers, sporting their matching Stonegate Farm shirts. It all looked very festive.

The first of our two lesson groups had the younger riders in it, including Connie. As I stood in the centre of the arena watching them all come in, I found myself holding my breath. Connie looked tense as she came through the door with Oscar, but she was holding onto those reins, not dropping them and dashing off to her Mom as she had done once or twice before. She caught my eye and smiled, and I breathed a sigh of relief. I smiled back, hoping it looked encouraging and not nervous, and gave her a "thumbs-up." She looked tiny next to the very tall Oscar who, while physically imposing, had the solid, go-slow attitude she needed to build her confidence. Together they strolled toward the first pylon, Oscar managing to keep his nose off her sleeve and next to her hand where it belonged. I felt myself relax a little.

One by one the riders completed their required leading pattern and handed their horses to the volunteers. A quick tack-check to make sure all girths were tight and bridles secure and we put the riders up using our oversized mounting block that made mounting manageable even for riders in wheelchairs. Now the volunteers would lead, with most riders accompanied by one or two "sidewalkers" as well. While the leader was in control of the horse, the sidewalkers were responsible for the rider: enforcing my directions as needed, encouraging, prompting, calming, and even holding the rider if required. For the most physically challenged riders, the assistance of sidewalkers is all that keeps them on their horses, and the job becomes exhausting if volunteers cannot be switched-out for a rest. But tonight's group was not that physically demanding, and the volunteers rarely had to hold the riders steady, except to trot.

The goals of therapeutic riding, as opposed to the kind of riding lessons provided by most riding schools, are as varied as the riders themselves. For some, it is the movement of the horse that provides the most important therapy. Human bodies that are limited in their own ability to move by illness or injury benefit greatly from sitting on a strong, large creature that moves underneath them, and that moves them, in turn. Joints and ligaments loosen up gently, and muscles grow stronger without too much strain. Balance improves as the horse's movement challenges the rider with changes of speed and direction. For others, like the riders in this evening's horse show, the therapy is more related to teaching focus, improving attention span and self-control by teaching riding skills. Maneuvering a horse through a zig-zag course of pylons or learning how to sit the bounciness of a trotting horse requires concentration, but the reward is pure fun. Riders learn without realizing they are learning, and the friendships developed with horses, volunteers and other riders go a long way toward teaching the inter-personal skills many of these youngsters find so difficult in other parts of their lives. A mutual love of horses is a great basis on which to start a conversation.

Much of what our young riders had learned, and were asked to demonstrate in the show, had to do with control of the horse. While the leader remained at the end of the lead rope (except for Helena, who would be allowed to "solo" without a leader), the riders steered the horses by pulling on the correct rein at the right time, asked them to "whoa" and "walk-on," and even "trot!" They had to sit up straight and look where they were going, keep their heels down and their shoulders back. Just like competitors at The Royal Winter Fair or the winter show circuit in Florida, they were expected to show good form while controlling their horses. But for these riders, the ultimate goals were far greater than just taking home that ribbon at the end.

We worked our way through mounted egg-and-spoon races, a "command class" requiring riders to walk, halt, turn and trot "on command," a modified trail class where riders steered through a course of poles and pylons, tossed stuffed animals into a bucket and rings onto a cone. We even had a walking race, won easily by the long-legged Oscar. This victory gave Connie an extra boost of confidence, and soon she was smiling broadly as she rode around the ring. To show their knowledge of grooming equipment the riders were sent on a scavenger hunt around the arena to collect a complete grooming kit before gathering in the centre of the ring to name the parts of horse, saddle and bridle they had learned each week. There were one or two tense moments as riders struggled to remember pommel (front of saddle) or withers (where the horse's neck joins his back), but the volunteers were shameless with their helpful hints and soon enough everyone was finished. I dismounted the riders, and presented each one with a ribbon (the colour matched the skill level each had been assigned to at the session's start), a t-shirt and a certificate of achievement they could hang on a wall. Cameras flashed as riders showed off proud trophies.

I had not expected so much excitement. The Mom of a rider in the second group told me her son had been nervous about remembering how to do everything. He had gone over all the homework assignments before coming to the horse show, and was even nervous about riding well enough to earn his ribbon. This surprised me, particularly since Paul was one of our regular riders, and had never shown this determination to achieve before. Even Helena, the young woman with years of riding experience, admitted to practicing the dressage test (pattern of movements to be performed in a specific order) I had asked her to perform as part of our show, on foot in her backyard. Twenty times or so! And James, he of the polished cowboy boots, outdid himself by posting at the trot (a rhythmical rising up and sitting down in time to the horse's movement) and naming obscure body parts like "poll" and "croup" that I had not even discussed in classes (evidently his school's library had a good book on the subject). He even explained to us that horses had feathers as well as hair – feathers being the long hair some horses, including our two Friesians, grew on their lower legs. He had even brought a photo of the Budweiser Clydesdale team to show us, with its eight gorgeous horses all sporting luxurious, spotlessly white feathers that covered their hooves and rippled when they walked.

Of course everyone "graduated." All riders had demonstrated the skills they had been assigned to learn, with several of them going well beyond what I had thought they could realistically achieve in our relatively short five weeks together.

After so much excitement, untying bows and shaking out braids seemed a little sad. Too final. Some of these riders, I knew, would not be back: their funding had run out and their families could not afford even the modest fees we had to charge to keep the horses fed and cared for. Everyone seemed reluctant to go: riders insisted on giving their horse that final stroke of the brush or dashed off to the feed room for "just one more carrot" to feed their horse. Volunteers swept and swept until the floor practically gleamed. Then they decided to stay and help me do the evening feeding, and then swept again because wisps of hay had fallen on the immaculate floor. I was tired. It had been a long day from the 5:30 feeding and turn-out in the morning through my classes at the college to this grand finale and late-night chores. Yet I felt a deep satisfaction, too, of something well accomplished. My horses had done me proud, and the little community that gathered in my stable two evenings a week to work with the horses and their special riders had given something to those children that they could get nowhere else. As the riders reluctantly tagged behind their parents through a soft summer night, out to their cars and then home, they were different than they had been five weeks ago when their program started. They had been changed in the way that only horses can change you.

2

God forbid that I should go to any
Heaven in which there are no horses.
(Robert Cunningham-Graham)

I had worked in high-tech my whole career, and in the hey-day
of the nineties I was fortunate enough to make enough money to buy my parents' house and small property, renovate the
house, build a small barn and paddocks, and eventually pay off
the mortgage. While my husband, Robert, and I had both spent
much of our careers traveling, now I was working from home
more, so it would be easy to look after the place. I would be able
to bring the elegant but aging Oscar home from the boarding
stable where I kept him. Karla, the young woman who coached
at the boarding stable, had a retired showhorse named North
who would come along to keep Oscar company. The old cam-
paigners would spend their days hanging out in the paddock,
going for an occasional ride in the outdoor ring, enjoying their
semi-retirement. They would keep the grass mowed and I would
have horses to play with right in my own backyard, instead of
driving to the boarding stable all the time. My younger son,
Christopher, could take riding lessons from Karla. Michael had

started riding, too, but of the two brothers, Christopher was far more motivated to ride. Still, both kids would learn what it meant to care for something other than themselves if they grew up on a "farm", no matter how small. Not a bad lesson for boys who would soon (too soon!) hit adolescence.

Setting up our modest six acres as a hobby farm was really about giving me more time with the horses. I had been riding most of my life, and always wanted to have horses at home. I felt that as long as someone else was doing the heavy lifting of horse-care – feeding, mucking stalls, turning out, deciding when to call the vet if a horse seemed ill or whether or not to put blankets on the horses before heading off to work on a January day – I wasn't truly a horsewoman. These seem like strange things to yearn for, but riding is like no other sport I know, set apart by the relationship between horse and rider. Much of that relationship is built from the ground rather than the saddle, through countless daily interactions between horse and human. Showing up for a couple of hours a day to groom and ride did not qualify. And while Robert had never owned a horse, he seemed excited by the idea of having them in the backyard, and maybe even starting to ride himself one day. So when my Dad decided to move back to Europe and the opportunity to buy the parental home came up, we jumped at it. We built an addition on the house where my Mother and our kids could have their bedrooms, and started thinking about barn design and fencing materials.

What started out in the planning stages as a basic little two-stall barn grew into a quite luxurious stable for six horses, complete with spacious aisles for grooming and room for tack and feed before a shovel even hit the ground. There were two paddocks and a hay-shed, and an outdoor sand-ring for riding. This last cost a small fortune to build because of all the trees and rocks that had to be removed first to clear a spot for it, and then for the tons of sand that had to be trucked in.

Through friends we were lucky enough to find a couple who were tearing down a barn and paddocks of their own to clear their property for development, and we bought much of the fence lumber, stall partitions and even feed buckets they would no longer need. Unfortunately their farm was 120 km away; the trips with rental trucks to pick up what we'd bought were long and tiring. Robert and I would get home at 7 or 8 in the evening and still be faced with unloading and cleaning up the truck and returning it to the rental company to avoid an extra day's charges. There were nights we questioned whether all the work was worth the bit of money we were saving by buying second-hand, but we persevered. By the time the paddocks were built, Robert and I had handled every one of the planks they were built from at least three times. If a horse broke one, we took it personally!

By the time we threw our "barn-warming" party in early summer, our little project had a great deal of money and sweat invested in it. Some blood, too, thanks to various construction injuries. As I drank wine with our friends on the back deck, watching Oscar and North wandering happily around their new paddock, I mused about the wonder of having horses at home. How satisfying to be able to look out my bedroom window and see horses. How lovely to hear their whinnies drift on the evening air. How perfectly marvelous to go to the barn late in the evening, bring them inside for dinner and stand for a few moments before shutting off the lights, listening to the quiet rustling of their feet as they moved around their stalls. There is no more peaceful sound in the world than this. I found myself sighing with contentment just thinking about it.

"So what are you going to put in those other gorgeous stalls?" I hadn't noticed Barb join me at the railing. The sound of her voice made me jump. I spilled some wine on the deck. Barb kept a lovely horse at Willowbrook, the boarding stable where Oscar had lived until just this week, and we'd often ridden together in the forest and fields behind the stable there.

"Wheel-barrows," I said. "Pitchforks. Hay."

"No way," she laughed. "I'll bet it takes you a year, tops."

"To do what?"

"To fill them all. With horses," she said with absolute confidence.

"No way," I said in turn, waving the idea away like an annoying fly. "What would I do with that many horses?"

Barb would have lost that bet, but only on the timing. Despite my arguments with Robert while we planned the barn that we DID NOT need six stalls, soon enough they were all full. Within two years my lovely paddocks would be grazed down to the roots by too many horses, and even the trees we'd left standing to provide the horses with shade had been stripped of their bark.

"You know the horse is closely related to the beaver, don't you?" my coach, Karla, joked as we watched Oscar daintily nibbling the last few bits of bark off a poplar. Several of the trees were already dead, unable to get nourishment up to their branches with no bark to cover their trunks. "At least they haven't gone after the fences. Yet," Karla added philosophically. Leave it to her to find the silver lining.

Soon we had more horses than stalls, and I had to put two of the youngsters on twenty-four-hour turn-out.

"Best thing in the world for them," my vet said when I told him. "Horses were not made to stand in stalls eating grain. They're meant to wander, grazing as they go."

I knew that, of course, but ours was not exactly a home on the range. The road that passed the front of our property had become a major commuter route as subdivisions sprouted all around us, and the road was busy twenty-four hours a day. Having horses outside at night with no one awake to watch them – with night-wandering critters who could frighten and drive them through a fence onto the road – in the dark – well, that cost me many hours of sleep. Many nights I'd wake up and worry, driven to sneak out of bed, from the bedroom, through the kitchen and into the dining room which offered a view of their paddock where I would stand shivering and peering pointlessly into the darkness, hoping to catch sight of them, safe and sound, on the right side of the fence. My stomach felt jumpy every morning when I headed to the barn, afraid of what I might find.

This was when I knew I had truly become a horsewoman. Every self-respecting horseperson I know has more horses than she has room for. The ends of aisles are blocked off to create additional stalls; ponies are kept two-per; horses stall-share, one staying in at night, the other during the day. This is where the horseperson's creativity shines! And the "mother" of this particular form of invention is the horseperson's other great talent – the ability to find horses that we simply MUST add to our collections. Like heat-seeking missiles, we are led to every "diamond-in-the-rough" that just needs a little polish, every sad-sack beast in need of a decent home. There are many ways to acquire horses one does not have need or room for, and all horsewomen will be familiar with several.

One way is to go into breeding. Besides having horses at home, a second dream of mine had been to breed and raise a foal. I'd been offered a foal once, when I'd first started riding, but wisely my parents had said "no." The romantic notion of having horse and rider "grow up together" usually turns to disaster. But the seed had been planted, and now that I had my own place, and Oscar was getting older with the ravages of a long show career beginning to reveal themselves in the form of arthritis and a creaky hip, perhaps the time was right. The old campaigner could hand on the torch, as it were; become mentor and paddock buddy, helping the young grow wise alongside the old.

So I leased a gorgeous Thoroughbred mare from my friends at Willowbrook, and bred her to a Dutch Warmblood stallion whose impeccable pedigree and famously calm temperament promised both athleticism and a good mind for his offspring. Of course I had chosen to ignore a fact I knew well: the mare is 60% of the equation in any breeding, and while Kelly was spectacular to look at, her temperament left something to be desired. She would walk all over me when I took her in from pasture at Willowbrook where she would continue to live with her herdmates during her pregnancy. In the barn she fretted and reared in the cross-ties, screaming for her friends, utterly unimpressed by her separation from them. More than herd-bound, she was stubborn and ornery, with little respect for humans and a very dominant attitude. She would bully and fuss, stepping on toes and body-checking humans into the wall at will. Ears perpetually pinned in surly warning and a sour look on her face, she was no joy to be around. Her promising competition career had supposedly been shortened by a ruthless trainer who had pushed her too hard, too fast, causing her to lose confidence and begin refusing jumps. After spending eleven months with Kelly awaiting my foal's birth, I began to wonder if there might be more to that particular story than I'd been told.

Olivia (registered name C'est la Vie) was born at 5 in the morning on a chilly day in May. I booked the day off work and headed to Willowbrook to spend my filly's first day on earth with her. She was beautiful. Big. Full of life. Whatever her other faults, Kelly made beautiful babies, and she was an excellent mother, taking good care of her foal but never over-protective. I was able to spend time in the stall with them, watching Olivia learn about her world: mom's tongue licking her, mom's udder with its warm milk, mom's soft nickering to tell her she was safe, the deep bed of straw with a strange human sitting in the corner watching, and stall walls that felt hard when she bumped into them. Her long legs would tangle sometimes and she fell in a heap, a surprised look on her face, and she would have to begin the long process of sorting out those miles of skinny legs, getting them organized under her and pushing herself back up to stand, swaying, tired from the effort.

On her second day of life she was allowed to go outside with her mother, and celebrated her freedom with a disjointed little canter that left her stranded with her front feet on one side of a prominent rock and her hind legs on the other. For a minute or two she could not figure out how to get all four feet on the same side of the obstacle. When she finally sorted herself out she trotted back to Kelly and stuck her nose under Mom's flank for a drink of milk, evidently quite worn out from the effort and starving. The humans watching from the paddock gate went crazy with love and admiration, as only horsepeople can, whenever there's a foal around. And this foal soon learned to play to her audience: never one to be a shrinking violet, Olivia delighted in showing off.

Since my agreement called for Olivia to stay at Willowbrook with Kelly until she was weaned, much of her early education fell to Karla, who managed Willowbrook's stable in addition to her coaching duties, and her assistant, Jamie. While I went to work and parent-teacher meetings at my sons' school and mucked out stalls at home, Jamie and Karla introduced Olivia to the other mares and foals, taught her how to wear a halter and allow herself to be led on a rope from stall to pasture. Only once Olivia was old enough to leave her mother and come live at our little farm would I take over as her primary care-giver, if not her teacher.

The "teacher" role would end up falling to Sahara, the big red mare who had meantime come to join our growing herd at home.

Having bred one beautiful foal, I began to have visions of a lucrative sideline breeding and selling sport horses – those big, expensive creatures you see at most dressage and hunter/jumper shows. My breeding-career delusion was aided and abetted by Robert, who saw the prices in the on-line ads and got heart palpitations.

"Fifteen thousand dollars?" he would read. "For a yearling? Cool!"

"Yes, but not just any yearling, Honey. His sire was an Olympic medalist."

"Yeah, but you can breed to a stallion like that, right?"

"Yes. For a price. And no guarantees the foal will turn out like its daddy."

"But it might."

So Sahara joined the herd. She was a well bred Hanoverian whose grandsire had been to the Olympics himself as part of a very successful show-jumping career in Europe. Her mother had both jumper and dressage genes in her bloodlines, and was a successful competitor on the A-circuit. She was famous for her easy-going manner and steadiness in the ring – traits she unfortunately failed to pass on to her daughter, Sahara. We had heard of Sahara through friends who knew her current owner. A young mare who'd had one foal already, they thought she would make a good foundation mare for a small breeding program like the one we were contemplating.

Clearly, the sparkling pedigree and strong recommendation warped my judgment. The Big Red Mare stood in her stall the day we first went to see her, with ears pinned back and an expression that immediately struck me as petulant.

"She's not used to being inside at this time of day," her owner, Cynthia, explained quickly, noticing me looking at the flattened ears. "She's really quite a lovely mare to work with. Usually."

I said nothing but noticed that the other mare Cynthia had brought in for another potential buyer to look at did not seem to have issues with coming into the barn in the middle of the day. She happily munched hay and blew gentle snorts through her nostrils at the curious humans standing by her stall, while Sahara stamped her foot in displeasure and swung her head from side to side like a shark looking for a tasty place to bite.

"Let's take her out so you can have a proper look," Cynthia said in an obvious attempt to distract me. Sahara towered over her, standing a solid 16'3 hands high, but looking even taller as she marched out of her stall, head held high. She fidgeted in the cross-ties, looking distinctly unhappy. She was six years old, but looked much younger, with the long-legged, gangly appearance of an immature horse. Bright chestnut with only a little white on her face and one leg, she was attractive but not stunning.

"She'll muscle up with work," Cynthia said, evidently reading my mind again. "She hasn't been in serious training since she had her first foal last year. It's stunning, by the way," she added, knowing my plans to eventually breed the mare.

I talked to the mare, rubbed her shoulder, fed her carrots, trying to get her to relax. No luck. She accepted the treats and toler- ated the attention but continued to fidget and fuss, calling to the horses outside and clearly unhappy. She tugged at the cross-ties, tossed her head angrily, and danced side-to-side and back-and-forth, forcing me to dance in turn to avoid having my feet stepped on. When I asked Cynthia to take her outside so we could see her move, the mare headed straight for her little group of friends and disappeared over a small hill. So much for seeing her move! All we knew was that she could gallop quickly.

"I can take her to a farm with an arena so you can try her," Cynthia said hopefully, brushing her clothes back into place after being dragged around by the big horse. It was winter, and the footing was too icy to ride in Cynthia's outdoor ring. "My daughter will be back from Europe next week. She can ride her for you first so you can see her go. Peggy – my daughter – has been in Germany training with (she named a famous dressage coach), but she gets back on Tuesday."

"I'll think about it," I said, ignoring the name-dropping. I had felt no connection to Sahara and did not intend to come back again. "I'll let you know."

"I don't like her," I told Robert as we were pulling out of Cynthia's driveway. "She's got an ugly attitude."

"It's only a first impression," he argued. "Why don't you at least ride her?"

And ride her we did. With Karla in tow we made the drive back to Cynthia's farm and then on to her friend's new dressage facility with a barn so stunning and perfectly kept it made you want to take your shoes off so you wouldn't dirty the floor. Cynthia's daughter introduced herself, and brought Sahara out of a stall. They had shipped her in the day before, she said, to let her get used to the place.

Peggy was even shorter than Cynthia, but Sahara seemed to respect her. Must be the German coaching, I thought. Accept no nonsense…

It worked right up until it was time to put on Sahara's bridle. Then The Big Red Mare threw her head in the air, nearly flinging Peggy across the barn. Sahara clenched her teeth and fought to avoid the bit. Being 16'3, this was not difficult. All she really had to do was keep her head held high and her nose in the air, her mouth out of reach. Peggy refused our offers of help, so we busied ourselves looking at the other horses in the barn. We did not want to embarrass the girl by watching her struggle. At one point from the corner of my eye I saw the mare lift Peggy completely off her feet and shake her like a Rottweiler with a new toy. Eventually though, Peggy prevailed. She was a little sweaty and her neatly coiffed hair was disheveled, but the mare was wearing her tack.

Once tacked up the mare seemed to settle, and only spooked once or twice at Robert videotaping her from the corner of the arena. My jaw dropped when Peggy put the mare into a trot. I heard Karla gasp beside me. The mare barely seemed to touch the ground. With long, floaty strides she flounced around the arena. Her feet snapped forward, her butt swung rhythmically, she hung suspended in the air between strides for impossibly long moments. "Look at me," she seemed to be saying with her body. "LOOK at ME!" Peggy smiled in the saddle. Anything that looked that good, I thought, must feel fantastic to ride.

"Wow," Karla said.

"Holy cow," I agreed.

"I didn't know a horse could move like that," Robert said, his eye glued to the camera display.

"Nice, isn't she?" Cynthia enthused, her spirits lifted by our reactions to her horse.

Karla and I both had our turns riding, and it took the better part of the long drive home to get the smiles off our faces. I had ridden some nice horses in my time, but never anything like this. What the mare lacked in charm and personality, she made up for with sheer physical talent.

"Put a few months' training on her," Karla said, "and you'll be ready to show."

I nodded. Clearly a horse of this caliber would have to be competed first, and then we could start breeding her. Maybe, with Olivia and Sahara as foundation mares, a nice little breeding operation was not out of the question?

But that "few months' training" would prove difficult to accomplish. Within a week of arriving at Willowbrook, where I decided to bring her so we could work more closely with Karla even if it meant paying board again for a while, Sahara popped a splint. Her right foreleg was hot, swollen and sore with a solid lump on the small splint bone which lies parallel to the large cannon bone below the horse's knee. While not a serious injury, it would need rest, restricted movement, and regular treatment with cold water and ice. Sahara would need to spend a couple of weeks in her stall, legs bandaged for support, and of course there would be no riding while the injury healed.

Stall rest, however, was not a concept Sahara was prepared to live with. When left inside after the rest of the horses went out to their paddocks for the day, Sahara threw a temper tantrum. She raced around the stall screaming, then reared as if attempting to climb out of the stall, front legs flailing at the partition. She would crash to all fours, then rear again, her pawing feet coming dangerously close to snagging on top of the divider. We watched in horror. She was a huge mare. What if she got her feet stuck up there? How would we ever get her down? She was working herself into a lather and was unquestionably in danger of hurting herself. Our attempts to calm her were ignored.

"I'll go get one of the other mares," Karla said after fifteen minutes or so, during which time Sahara's tantrum had kept escalating. "Maybe she'll settle down if she has a friend in the barn with her."

Now I KNEW it was serious. It was not like Karla to make concessions of this sort to any horse's bad behaviour. She returned a few minutes later with Kitten, one of Sahara's paddock buddies, and put her in the stall next to Sahara's. The big mare stopped spinning and touched noses with Kitten through he bars. The two mares stood close, blowing air into each other's nostrils. The humans breathed a collective sigh of relief.

The brief greeting finished, Sahara wheeled around and reared again, lunging at the front of her stall. Within a few minutes, her frantic behaviour had infected Kitten, and now both mares were upset, though only one was threatening to take the barn apart. Sahara.

"We could sedate her," Karla offered, wincing as the mare bounced off a wall and screamed angrily.

"Or let her wear herself out," Jamie said.

"Or we could just put her outside with her friends. She'll get more "rest" out there," I said.

The two women looked relieved. Putting Sahara outside meant contradicting the vet's orders and they hadn't wanted to suggest it. But sometimes, common sense needs to prevail. We snapped lead-shanks onto the mares' halters, led them to their paddock, and watched them calmly walk to their hay and begin to munch. Were these the same hellcats who'd just been screaming in the barn?

The splint healed just as quickly without stall rest, and Willowbrook's barn was still standing.

Thankfully there was no repeat performance the next time Sahara was confined to a stall, following her colic surgery just a few months later. Perhaps the long, stapled incision in her belly gave her second-thoughts about rearing up and trying to dismantle her stall, or perhaps she had simply settled in at Willowbrook by then and decided it was OK to do as she was told. Whatever the case, she was a model patient the second time around, and did not try to kill us even when we began to hand-walk her gradually as she recovered. Soon she was able to go out on pasture again, but she'd undergone major abdominal surgery and it would be months before she could return to regular work. It made no sense to pay expensive board at a show-barn for a horse that could not be ridden, so I brought Sahara home to join Oscar and North. Before long Olivia was old enough to be weaned from Kelly, and she, too, joined the little herd in my back yard. Now there were four.

Olivia became very attached to Sahara once they were both at our little barn. She must have come to see her as a substitute mother, and Sahara seemed to enjoy the role. I was glad that the young filly had found a friend among the adults, but I was soon to find out that the relationship was perhaps a little too close.

I had taken Sahara out for a ride in the sand ring. Her recovery from surgery had been steady and uneventful, and the vet had cleared me to begin the slow road back to conditioning and training. I had just mounted the mare when I noticed that Olivia was running around in the paddock, looking for her friend. I had purposely left her in the paddock nearest the sand ring so she could see Sahara while we worked, but apparently this was not good enough. She had the geldings for company, too, just on the other side of the fence, but I could see Olivia was beginning to panic as her laps of the paddock increased in speed and her whinnies took on a shriller tone. Then, for reasons known only to herself, Olivia took off at a gallop toward the barn whose double-dutch doors opened into the paddock she was in. Without slowing her headlong rush the filly attempted to clear the closed bottom half of the doors. It was a good four feet to the top of those doors and she nearly made it. She did manage to get her front end over. But sadly, her hind end did not quite clear the doors, and she got stranded: front feet on the barn floor on one side of the door, hind legs dangling like strings of spaghetti on the other, unable to touch the ground.

I'd watched this scenario develop in horror from the sand ring, and then I was off Sahara in a flash, dragging her by the reins behind me, through the sand ring gate and toward the paddock, terrified of what the filly might do to herself as she struggled to get free. I twisted my damaged knee (two torn ligaments courtesy of a ski crash), and ended up hopping part of the way, Sahara dragging in my wake, her head thrown back and ears laid flat against her neck, obviously unimpressed with my thoughtless treatment of her Hanoverian-ness. At the moment, though, my only concern was for the stranded filly.

Had I been less hopped up on adrenalin and panic I might have stopped before reaching Olivia and appreciated the humour of the scene: two absurdly long, skinny legs dangling beneath an equally skinny butt from the top of the half-door; unmoving, unhurt, no body or head visible at all. Miraculously Olivia had chosen not to struggle or try to fight her way out of her predicament, so she was undamaged and quite still. Simply hanging there.

And here's where the adrenalin came in handy. I grabbed those skinny hind legs and pushed, shoving the big filly over the door the rest of the way into the barn where she landed bewildered and whole, not a scratch on her. My knee was not so lucky. It throbbed and ached for days while I hobbled around doing chores.

Not satisfied to let Olivia have all the glory, and in her on-going attempts to disrupt her training, Sahara decided it was her turn to have a go at the farm structures only a week or two later.

Since I now had two geldings and two mares at home, I decided to separate them by gender. Many horse farms separate their herds of geldings and mares. Things are often more peaceful this way. So while I had integrated Sahara into North and Oscar's mini herd at first, now that she had a second female for company, I decided to try gender-split turn-out. Besides, my two paddocks shared a common fence-line, so nothing would separate Sahara from the two geldings but a row of oak planks. This would not be a radical change in her life.

Sahara did not approve. When she found the gate between the two paddocks closed for the first time and Oscar and North on the other side of it, she galloped, screaming, down the length of the paddock along the offending fence-line. Reaching the end, she spun around, and ran screaming back again. And again. Gaining speed and growing more frantic with every trip up and down the field. Once she spun so quickly at the bottom of the paddock that her feet flew out from under her and she crashed to the ground. My heart stopped, but in a flash she was up again, apparently unhurt and angry. A big horse that's on the verge of being out of control is an awe-inspiring sight, but not one that fills one's heart with gladness. You just know that if something happens, it will be spectacular. Most likely, it will be spectacularly bad.

Nothing did. Eventually she stopped running. Perhaps realizing that the geldings who'd initially jogged up and down the fence-line in sympathy beside her were no longer paying any attention to her, Sahara slowed down and then stopped. She touched noses with Olivia who had been vainly trying to keep up with her, uncertain what her "mom" was doing but determined to do the same. Then the two mares dropped their heads and began to graze.

Relieved, I ducked under the fence and walked to where they were eating. I ran my hands over the mare's body and legs, checking for injuries. She was sweaty but unhurt, and as it was a mild day I decided to leave her where she was to cool off gradually on her own. Thinking the worst was over, I headed back to the house to finish a newsletter I had started writing for work.

My office window had a limited view of the southern paddock, and I enjoyed being able to look up and see the horses if they happened to wander into view. It was a lovely sight: Oscar, his nose always to the ground, shuffling slowly around like Eeyore; North expertly threading his way among the little stand of trees despite having only one eye; Sahara trotting majestically around them like the alpha mare she was... Sahara? I bounced out of my office chair. What was Sahara doing in the paddock with the boys?

I rushed outside in time to see Olivia, whinnying to her adoptive mother, finally get the nerve to jump over the gate Sahara had pulled off its hinges and left lying at a weird angle between the two paddocks. Thankfully Olivia had cleared the gate safely and galloped over to the adults, quite distressed at having been left behind. Sahara nuzzled her apologetically, then returned to the business of herding the boys to the spot where SHE wanted them to be, under the trees. They complied without arguing.

The gate was dangerous, dangling from its latch, so I righted it and managed to hang it back on its hinges first. Then I went to the mare to do yet another damage assessment. This time the news was worse. Sahara's right front leg had several shallow cuts. More alarmingly, it was hot to the touch and beginning to swell. She flinched when I touched it and seemed reluctant to put her weight on it. I led her to the barn and called the vet.

Ed shook his head a little as he examined the mare's leg.

"This one sure knows how to get herself in trouble, doesn't she?" Ed was Willowbrook's vet as well as ours, and had treated Sahara's popped splint and her bout with colic while she was there. "We'd better x-ray this to make sure nothing's broken."

Thankfully the damage was only to the soft tissue, and not terribly serious at that. More cold-water therapy and wrapping in supportive bandages of the sort Sahara was becoming well accustomed to, and my mare would soon be fit again. She must have stuck her foot through the gate somehow and pulled, lifting the heavy gate clear off its hinges. Naturally, I did not try to segregate the herd again. It worked better that way in the end. If I wanted to take Oscar or Sahara out for a ride, the other horses would keep each other company; no need to worry about one horse being left alone.

We now had a nice working arrangement. Four of my stalls had horses in them, and I filled the other two with hay and shavings to save me the daily trip out to the storage shed. Oscar was semi-retired now, going for an occasional ride with me or one of my kids – nothing strenuous – just keeping him from losing too much muscle-tone and his joints from stiffening up more than they already had. His long show career had taken its toll. Years of jumping fences had damaged his joints and stressed his ligaments. He came out of his stall in the mornings like the old man he was – stiff and creaky. The more we could get him to move, the better.

Oscar seemed pleased with semi-retirement, but we did make one concession to his former status as a show-horse; he got to wear horseshoes on his front feet. He did not need them. Oscar's feet were strong and healthy and never prone to cracking, but if we pulled those shoes off he would hobble around the paddock like a cripple, refusing to take a regular step. Perhaps it was one of those vanities – like a faded and forgotten movie star who refuses to leave her house without full hair and make-up just in case she's recognized or photographed – so the former show horse needed his shoes to connect him to his former glory.

"Some horses take a while to adjust to going barefoot," my farrier explained, chuckling as he watched Oscar's "I can't walk barefoot" routine. "The feet start to splay out a little after years of being confined by shoes, the soles get closer to the ground and sometimes bruise before they toughen up. But unless a horse has bad feet, which Oscar certainly doesn't, they're fine in a few weeks."

He looked at Oscar again and rubbed his hand across the top of his balding head.

"On the other hand, some horses are… They're…"

"Wimps?" I offered.

"Good word. Yes."

So Oscar was allowed to keep his shoes. I tended to indulge the old man. He'd spent most of his life obediently performing in the hunter ring, jumping whatever he was told to jump, and winning many ribbons. He deserved an occasional break. And besides, he looked so pitiful when barefoot that I worried passersby would call the SPCA and report me for cruelty. Bad enough I "blind-folded" my horses (several recently transplanted city types had actually pulled into the driveway, demanding to know why I did that to my horses. I had to explain that the blind-folds were flymasks, see-through, and designed only to keep the bugs out of the horses' eyes).

Oscar was also terrified of water, because water, as horses well know, can swallow you right up. Even if it's just a puddle in the middle of the trail. This was a lesson Oscar had evidently learned early in life and never forgotten. In a way, it was the reason I was able to own him now, for Oscar had been bred in Ireland of excellent steeple-chasing stock, and intended to be a high-level Eventer. But Eventers are not only expected to charge fearlessly through water on cross-country courses, they are expected to jump into and out of it. Some of the most dramatic images from eventing competitions like Rolex or Badminton are those of horse and rider splashing through the water obstacles. I am certain that whoever had spent the money to import Oscar to Canada and train him had tried hard to convince him that this would be a fun thing to do, but apparently with no success. The best I was ever able to do with him myself was to walk through an occasional puddle and just barely dip his toes in the lake while his friends happily went swimming with their riders.

So Oscar had been made into a show hunter. His job now would be to jump over relatively small obstacles in a quiet, comfortable, easy-going manner that was meant to demonstrate his suitability for riding out with hounds. In the show-ring his lack of bravery was less of an issue and the worst he was ever asked to do with respect to water was jump OVER it – an obstacle he never failed to clear with room to spare. And then one night his portable stall had flooded at a show he had been shipped to. That must have been the worst night of his life: he was found in the morning huddled in the one tiny corner of the stall that had stayed dry, his feet bunched under him, his eyes bugging out in fear of the encroaching flood.

When he'd hurt his hip in a paddock accident and been retired from the show-ring, I was able to buy him for a reasonable price. He was beautiful: a 17-hand dark bay Irish Thoroughbred who exuded the kind of aristocratic refinement that only Thoroughbreds are capable of. But beneath the elegant skin beat the mushy heart of a coward. Oscar could not be left alone. His separation anxiety was so pronounced that he would begin screaming and worrying the moment the horse in the stall beside him was taken outside. The barn could be full, but if the neighbouring stall was empty, Oscar was worried. On trail rides he would spook and bolt more than most, and sights as apparently harmless as a herd of Percheron horses on the other side of a fence could unhinge him, turning him into a quivering mass of equine fear. To my mind, Oscar's neuroses only made him more endearing.

In the paddock, Oscar was best friends with Karla's old horse, North, a lovely little Thoroughbred gelding whose only behavioural issue was a passionate hatred of the vet. Any vet. The fear probably came from the unpleasantness he'd had to endure when he lost his eye. No one could quite figure out how that had happened. North had come in from his paddock at Willowbrook where Karla worked, with severe damage to his left eye. An immediate call to the vet and diligent care were unable to save the eye, and Karla eventually made the difficult decision to have what was left of the eye removed.

I had ridden a one-eyed horse a few times at the "rent-a-horse" ranch where I'd had my earliest experiences on horseback, paying $1.25 per hour to ride on one of a string of nose-to-tail horses through the trail system on a large property. The one-eyed horse was an old pinto named Pablo, and his empty eye-socket was a shocking feature in his thin, old-horse face. I remember always trying to avoid his blind side, both to keep from spooking him (what they cannot see tends to frighten horses), as well as to avoid having to look at the gaping hole. I'd expected the same when North came back to Willowbrook from the clinic after his surgery, but he looked surprisingly normal. The eyeball had been replaced with silicone and the eyelids sewn shut. You had to get very close to notice the missing eye. And he adapted to his semi-blindness quickly, too, even managing to navigate our treed paddocks easily once Karla moved him to our farm to live with Oscar. I never saw him bump into a tree once, and within a few days he felt confident enough to canter through the thicket.

The only fright North ever gave me was the day he collapsed while eating hay just outside the barn door. We were eating dinner, and since the dining room of our house overlooked the paddock, I liked to glance outside from time to time and see what the horses were doing. That particular evening I was enjoying my spaghetti, chatting with Michael and Christopher about their day at school, when I suddenly saw North fall to the ground. Not all the way to the ground. His front legs had seemed to give out, and he'd crashed forward while his hind legs remained standing, his butt swaying strangely. I nearly choked on my garlic bread as I threw down my fork and raced outside, the kids hot on my heels. By the time we reached the paddock, North was on all four feet again, apparently none the worse for wear. I checked him over and immediately called Karla.

"Oh," she said, sounding sheepish. "Did I forget to mention he has a slight case of narcolepsy? He falls asleep like that. The fall usually wakes him up. I thought I'd told you. Sorry."

Yes, that would have been good information to have earlier, I thought, but no harm done. What's the point of having horses around if they can't scare the breath right out of you from time to time? This, after all, was what I had longed for. This was life with horses.

3

Wherever man has left his footprint in the
long ascent from barbarism to civilization, we
will find the hoofprint of the horse beside it.
(John Trotwood Moore)

By the time our little backyard barn had been built and Oscar, North, Olivia and Sahara had come to live there, I had been riding horses for nearly thirty years. For much of that time, I had been at least peripherally aware of therapeutic riding. Articles would appear from time to time in some of the horse magazines I liked to read, and even in the daily papers, describing one program or another that was offering riding opportunities for special-needs riders; usually children, usually with physical disabilities. Inevitably there would be a photo of a smiling youngster on a horse, a wheelchair left behind in the background, and a story about newly-discovered freedom on the back of a horse.

I could understand that smile on the youngster's face without even reading the story. Few things in life compare to the feeling of sitting on a horse. The great animal's power. His willingness to share his strength and grace with a mere human. How many times would that thrill be multiplied for a rider who was confined to a wheelchair? I wondered.

I always felt good after reading those stories. Glad that good people were doing good work with their horses. Grateful for their efforts, the way I was grateful for the rescue groups that cared for sick and starving horses or rounded up stray cats or collected money for the food bank. I'd usually jot down the organization's name and location, planning to call them up sometime. Volunteer. Give a donation. Some day. When I had the time or money…

Then one day as I was eating lunch at my desk and reading yet another horse magazine, I came across a different kind of "horse therapy" story. This one described a farm in the United States that offered a kind of haven for kids who were fighting life-threatening illnesses. The farm was a place for these children and their families to go where they could forget about hospitals and medications and treatments and surgeries, and all the things no child should have to deal with. It was a place where no one told the children what they could not do. They were free to just BE for a while. Ride a horse if they wanted to, or just sit and watch the horses in their paddocks. Go into the barn-yard and let a goat climb on their lap. Pat the barn cat and listen to it purr. In other words, do all the things that those of us lucky enough to be involved with horses and stables took for granted and derived so much joy from in our daily lives.

"Wow," I thought. "Imagine being able to offer that kind of experience to people."

So how do I start?

I visited the website of CanTRA (Canadian Therapeutic Riding Association), and from there began my research.

I found out that there was some evidence of riding being used for therapeutic purposes as far back as Ancient Greece, around 600 BCE. Once I got my head around that astonishing fact, though, I decided that it probably went back even further than that, and just lacked documentation. After all, how long would it have taken, once a human mounted a horse, to notice how much better riding could make you feel?

Modern therapeutic riding programs date back to the late 1800s and a French physician named Cassaign who prescribed riding for patients suffering from neurological disorders and joint pain. Dr. Cassaign had been taking advantage of what current medical practice has come to understand more fully: that the motion of a walking horse mirrors the motion of a human walk, and moves the rider's body in exactly the same way. This movement can improve the mobility of stiff joints and improve the strength of muscles. It improves co-ordination and balance as well, since the horse's movement challenges the rider to follow the motion of the horse.

Those who are not riders like to joke that riding only provides exercise for the horse. Clearly, they've never tried to ride over a course of jumps, master the sitting trot, or teach a horse an advanced dressage movement. Any of these can leave the rider as exhausted as the horse. But even a simple walk can be demanding, especially if your riding muscles are not fit – or you spend your days in a wheelchair.

I tried an experiment that a therapeutic riding instructor suggested to me, and closed my eyes while riding around the sand ring on Oscar one day. By shutting out the distractions around me I was able to focus only on his movement, and mine. I became aware of things that had become second-nature over decades of riding: how my seat-bones moved independently, following his strides beneath me, pushing first one hip forward, then the other. How my spine moved, my lower back loosened up and flowed, my stomach muscles absorbed the motion and kept my upper body still. My legs had to wrap around his swaying barrel, relaxed and yet able to exert pressure independently of each other as I asked for changes of direction, circles, halts. His movements telegraphed back to me the details of the terrain he walked on, every dip a valley when it came unseen and unexpected, demanding an instant response from my own body to keep from toppling forward.

Now I was hooked. I found NARHA (North American Riding for the Handicapped Association) next, and dug into their website, too. One of the press releases there described a program called "Horses for Heroes," which offered therapeutic riding for injured veterans returning from Afghanistan and Iraq. I found some linked stories, and they all talked about the same things: how riding was helping the veterans – many of whom had lost limbs and experienced horrific trauma – both physically and emotionally. Learning new skills again. Allowing themselves to be helped in their efforts (many of the volunteers were veterans themselves). Getting outdoors and away from the hospital. Experiencing challenges and successes. Connecting emotionally with horses and helpers and other riders, too.

Even this program had a precedent in history, I would soon find out. Something quite similar had been run at a hospital just outside of Oxford, England, for wounded soldiers returning from World War One.

And then I read about Lis Hartel, a Danish equestrian who did more to raise the profile of therapeutic riding than perhaps anyone else in history. Stricken by polio in 1943 and paralyzed in her legs, hands and left side by the illness, she went on to not only deliver a healthy daughter with whom she'd been pregnant at the time, but also to fight against the effects of that horrible disease with incredible determination. Although her doctors had advised her never to ride again, she returned to the sport she loved and made it part of her rehabilitation. While it might have been easier to simply accept her new physical limitations and live a sedentary life, Lis Hartel fought back.

The 1952 Olympics in Helsinki marked the first time that Dressage competition at the Games would be open to civilians, not just commissioned military officers as had been the norm until then. Four women took the opportunity to compete against the men. Lis Hartel was one. She went on to win the silver medal at those Games, and to repeat that performance at the 1956 Games as well. Her illustrious career would include a World Championship, and 7 Danish National Dressage Championships. Perhaps just as importantly, she would inspire disabled riders and other athletes, as well as doctors, therapists, coaches and many, many others around the world. She traveled extensively, teaching and promoting, raising funds for polio associations and therapeutic riding groups. Her efforts helped to popularize therapeutic riding in many countries outside her native Denmark.

By the 1960s, Canada and the U.S. each had at least one riding centre dedicated to therapeutic riding, and soon CanTRA and NARHA would be formed.

I joined CanTRA, and started looking for a program in my area where I could volunteer and learn more. There was none. The closest I could find was a small but very interesting program run by a riding instructor and a physical therapist about an hour's drive from me. I called them up, liked what I heard, and started driving down once a week to spend the day volunteering.

That fall, I went to CanTRA's annual conference. One of the presenters was a clinical psychologist who worked primarily with teens. She had been using horses increasingly in her work, and eventually moved her practice out the office entirely and into her stable. She showed videos of several of her sessions, where teens learned to work through their issues by working with a horse. It was remarkable.

In one video, a young woman who had been sexually abused and lacked trust, confidence and self-esteem was paired up with a nervous, willful horse in a small riding arena, and asked to make him perform a few basics: walk, trot, turn on command. The young woman looked tiny and lost in the middle of the ring, the horse circling her warily. The horse mirrored all the girl's uncertainties, refusing to do what she asked, unwilling to take direction from her. With the psychologist's help, over many sessions, the young woman came to see how her own body language was reflected back to her by the body language of the horse, and how, by making subtle changes to what she "said" with her gestures and her posture she could influence this large, strong creature and have him comply with her requests. She was learning that she could in fact be the one who was in control. As the horse began to respond, her confidence grew. She seemed amazed at her ability to direct another living being. Once she gained the horse's trust, he happily did as he was told, and the young woman began to smile.

Another video showed a young man who had very different problems: ones of anger and the need to dominate. He was paired up with a horse who would not allow himself to be bullied or pushed around. The young man was sent into a large paddock to catch the horse, put a halter on him, and bring him into the stable. His aggressive approach did not play well, and the horse simply turned and trotted away with a swish of his tail. The young man followed that horse around, trying to outsmart, outmanouever, outlast him. The more angry and determined he became to catch the horse, the more determined the horse became to elude him. The odds were stacked against the human. The game went on for over an hour. The young man finally caved in and asked for help. The therapist suggested a different approach – inviting the horse to co-operate instead of demanding his submission, and the gelding at last stood still. Halter finally on, the horse happily followed the young man out of the paddock. A connection had been made.

I could hardly believe what I was learning. There were programs for grieving children. Empowerment workshops for women.

Programs for prison inmates and at-risk teens. Therapy for individuals diagnosed with arthritis, autism, cerebral palsy, ADD, ADHD, fetal alcohol syndrome…

Sometimes the benefits were physical. Borrowing the horse's strength and movement to help a compromised human body. Sometimes they were cognitive. Teaching skills in an unstressful, fun way. And sometimes they were spiritual. Relying on the horse's innate generosity of spirit, his kindness, his acceptance of people regardless of their disabilities, his honesty and trust. For those who find it difficult to connect with other humans, the horse can be a bridge. For those who cannot focus, communicate, tolerate change – the horse can teach without seeming to teach anything at all. For those with anxieties and fears, the horse can calm. For those who fear failure, the horse offers the opportunity to try without fear of judgment.

In the history of man and horse, the relationship has always been one-sided. The horse gives. The human takes. From source of food to more efficient means of hunting; from transportation to agriculture to industry and warfare, the horse has helped to build our world. Each time the horse has been replaced by something more efficient – steam-engines, tractors, cars, jets, tanks – cynics would declare the species obsolete. And every time, we would find a new use for the horse.

"I wouldn't spend more than five dollars on the best horse in America," declares Charles Howard early in the movie *Seabiscuit*.

A visionary who was quick to recognize the potential of the car,

Howard made his fortune selling Buicks and grandly declared the horse to be finished. Certainly, as transporation, for the most part it was. And yet even this hard-nosed modernist succumbs to the power of the horse by the end of Seabiscuit's story, recognizing in his little racehorse the remedy to heal a country and a people ravaged by the Depression. The diminutive horse, on whom so many others had given up, went on to beat the odds. Fight back. Overcome. The way the country and the world would eventually overcome, too, and fight their way back to prosperity and hope.

Only horses can do that. Because, throughout our long history together, the bond between man and horse has always been about more than mere utility. There is so much more to horses than their physical ability to carry us around and pull our ploughs.

I saw proof of this on my very first day of volunteering. What I saw when I parked my car in the shade of the beautiful old maple trees lining the driveway was a very young girl – no more than 4 or 5, lying in the deep soft grass with another young girl – quite obviously a twin sister – sitting beside her. When the girl who was seated jumped up to chase a barn cat that had wandered into view, her sister flipped over onto her stomach and chased hope-lessly after them, using only her arms for propulsion, her lower body dragging limply behind. Soon sister and cat were out of sight and the little girl was crying.

Not even the comfort of her mother's arms could console her. Then Elaine, the riding instructor, appeared, leading a small horse tacked up with a large saddle pad and the type of surcingle acrobats use for vaulting on horseback: a padded leather strap that circles the horse's body and has two solid handles at the top. Vaulters use these for doing handstands and fancy flips. The young girl I could not take my eyes off used them to balance herself as she sat on the horse. Her own legs were of no use to her (due to an incompletely developed spine, I would eventually learn), but the horse's legs worked just fine, thank you, and suddenly she was bigger and faster and more powerful than her twin sister, and faster even than that elusive cat. And now she was smiling, sitting on top of the world because she was sitting on top of a horse.

The description I had found on Elaine's website as I searched for the best place to start my hands-on learning didn't do this program justice. It talked clinically about rider size and weight restrictions (the stable didn't have a mechanical lift, so Elaine had to lift disabled riders onto the horses' backs herself), and the types of disabilities Elaine and her physiotherapist partner, Debbie, specialized in working with. It talked in the language of the doctor's office and physiotherapy clinic: range of motion, muscle tone and spasticity. It described outcomes and prognoses. What it delivered, however, as I plainly saw before me, was magic.

4

*And Allah took a handful of southerly
wind, blew his breath over it, and created
the horse. 'Thou shalt fly without wings,
and conquer without any sword.'*
(Bedouin Legend)

Between the semi-retired Oscar, the injury-prone but mostly rideable Sahara and the weanling Olivia in need of training in the basics of good horse behaviour, and looking after Karla's horse, North, I wasn't exactly short of horses to play with. Working full-time and volunteering with Elaine and Debbie's therapeutic riding program, I had plenty to do. I wasn't looking for another horse – but then, they rarely come along when you particularly need them.

The phone rang. It was Harry Witteveen, speaking with a Dutch accent that decades of living in Canada had not managed to erase.

"So, was it a stud-colt you were looking for?"

I had forgotten about even making the call months earlier. That was before I had been talked out of buying a Friesian on the grounds that they were too expensive. Sale videos of gorgeous, round-bodied black horses with flowing kinky manes and tails and "feathers" at their feet had been replaced by video after video of big-moving, dressage-show-ready European warmblood mares and culminated in my purchase of Sahara, The Big Red Mare. Of course Sahara ended up costing nearly as much as a good Friesian would have, and that was BEFORE all the vet bills she'd manage to run up, but she was an investment in the future, after all. A future mother of $15,000-yearlings… A Friesian would have been a mere indulgence…

I had been drawn to the Friesian breed by a variety of things, not least of all their stunning looks. With their powerful build, arched necks and elegant heads they were completely different from the sport horses currently in fashion which were all minor variations on the same warmblood theme. The Friesian was like a Bentley in a parking lot full of BMWs and Mercedes-Benzes. Not *better*, necessarily, but *different*. And beneath the stunning exterior, most Friesians harboured a particularly generous, people-loving soul. More than most, these horses were kind and gentle, easy to train and more than willing to please.

Like the Andalusian (Rasa Pura Espanol), Lusitano and Lipizzaner, with whom it shares many common traits, the Friesian is an ancient breed. He has been war horse, carriage horse, competition "trotter" and light draft, working the fields of his native Holland. Replaced by modern artillery, tractors, cars, and faster trotters like the American Standardbred and Russian Orlov, the Friesian has nearly become extinct more than once. But always he has been brought back from the brink by a handful of dedicated breeders who loved the great black horse. In North America, Harry Witteveen is one of those breeders.

"I beg your pardon?" I stammered, trying to remember who this slightly familiar-sounding voice belonged to.

"The Friesian horse," Harry repeated patiently. "You were looking for a colt?"

"Yes," I said, finally remembering the conversation. I had always preferred riding geldings. It had been a colt I had been looking for when my search for Oscar's replacement had begun.

"When do you want to come see them? I have some yearlings. And one young one almost ready to be weaned."

"How about Thursday?" I shocked myself by saying. Hadn't I just spent a small fortune on one of those long-legged, floaty-gaited warmbloods everyone told me I should own? And didn't I have another one that was five months old, all legs and potential? These mares could keep me busy for years.

"Is eleven o'clock OK?" I asked.

"Fine. See you Thursday."

There was nothing rational about the decision.

I dragged Karla along once again, though in truth she didn't need too much convincing. Of all the people I knew, she was the only one who'd actually ridden a Friesian, having competed her boss's mare for a couple of years at the barn she had managed before coming to Willowbrook. Despite the snide comments of some of her fellow dressage competitors (like – "shouldn't there be a cart attached to the back of that horse?") they did pretty well when they found a judge who was willing to look beyond the breed and consider the horse. Those were the days before Baroque horses like Friesians and Andalusians became trendy themselves, of course. Today Friesians can be found at all levels of dressage competition and no wonder – one look at the old paintings and sketches of dressage masters who invented the art, and it's not hard to see that short-coupled, round-bodied Baroque horses were what the classical foundation was built on.

I also brought Robert along on the trip. I suppose at some level I wanted him to talk me out of this.

Harry's farm was neat and tidy, with a lovely carriage house that turned out to be stocked with some spectacular vehicles. Harry competed his horses in driving classes – he had been a regular at the Royal Agricultural Winter Fair in Toronto for decades -- and had collected some beautiful rigs to showcase them in. We could have spent a full day in that carriage house, but there were horses to be seen, and horses win out over carriages every time.

We went to the barn first, where Harry proudly showed off some brood-mares and a handful of youngsters in training, rhyming off complicated pedigrees and giving us a crash course in Friesian geneology. Breeding – good breeding, which actually tries to improve the breed – is always a complicated business, but with the Friesian it's that much harder. Having been virtually wiped out, the breed was left with a small gene pool. Avoiding excessive in-breeding while maintaining the purity of the breed is a challenge.

After the barn tour, we headed outside, past a very unhappy but spectacular looking young stallion screaming and whirling around in a round-pen, his long, wavy mane and tail sweeping in his wake, nostrils flared, neck arched and gleaming with sweat. He was magnificent, but not exactly the picture of Friesian tranquility I had been expecting.

"He's about to start his training," one of Harry's assistants explained. "We let the youngsters run as a herd until they're three, so he's kind of upset about leaving his buddies. But he'll calm down in a day or two."

At the time I had some doubts about this statement, but that was before I truly came to know the Friesian horse.

We stopped at a large, fenced sand ring and watched as Harry's staff brought several yearlings from a nearby pasture and turned them loose. The youngsters frolicked and showed off as a trainer stood in the centre, urging them on with a lungeing whip. All were lovely.

Given that all Friesians are black – no other colour is permitted, and no white markings are allowed – as well as having very similar conformation in accordance with the breed standard, I had wondered how Harry could tell them all apart. With more than sixty horses on the farm, many of them youngsters who ran in a herd on pasture twenty-four-hours a day, how could he possibly know which horse was which? Did each horse wear a halter with its name on it? It turned out I had been thinking much too low-tech. Harry and his daughter Carol came to the sand ring armed with a microchip reader and a neat folder filled with papers. Scanning the microchip in each yearling's neck and referring to computer print-outs, they were quickly able to look up names and pedigrees with absolute accuracy.

While yearlings tend to be gangly and awkward, these colts were beautiful. They were also rather expensive, and my budget had been badly dented by the purchase of Sahara. Making a few mental notes on the various individuals, I asked to see the baby, hoping for a more affordable price.

Henk was barely four months old and apparently not very used to people. He hugged his dam's side as she was brought into the ring, and did his best to stay on the side *away* from the humans. Mostly, it looked like the small, powerful mare had eight legs. But the trainer expertly managed to turn the pair and send them walk / trot / cantering around the ring so we could see the baby and the mother, too.

"Wow," I heard Karla say beside me. "He has a great canter."

Judging a baby's movement took years of very specific experience I didn't have, but he certainly seemed nicely balanced and strong, with well-formed legs, the typical upright neck carriage of a Friesian, and dark, lively eyes. He moved with nice long strides, having no trouble keeping pace with his dam.

The mare was quite small, and that worried me a little. I'm tall and long-legged and tend to look ridiculous on a small horse. I voiced my concern to Harry.

"He'll finish 16 hands," the old horseman replied, as sure of himself as if he'd just told me what he would be eating for dinner that night. I had no reason to doubt him, and lacked the "Friesian" experience to know if what he said was reasonable. In this, as in everything else, Harry would be proven right. Henk would stand 16 hands high at the withers once he matured. Exactly.

Karla clearly approved, and the price was as good as I could expect for a quality Friesian. When you buy a rare breed, you're entering a seller's market, and have very little negotiating leverage. I had scoured the websites and magazines for months while Friesian-shopping earlier in my new-horse search, and most of the prices had made me feel faint. I had two things going for me, though: it was fall, and most people prefer to buy in spring or summer when they'll have lots of nice weather to play with their new beasties, and Henk was a baby. His price was much lower than it would have been for a horse that was ready to ride. Of course that was a false savings, since weanlings do nothing but eat, poop, get themselves in trouble and cost money in basic upkeep and vet and farrier bills for years before they become useable riding horses. And while I had an available stall in the barn, I also had The Old Man, The Big Red Mare, and Olivia. How many horses did one person need, anyway? I would have to go home and think this over.

"OK," I said instead. "When can I come pick him up?"

Karla and Robert looked at me in shock. While I hate shopping and tend to be an impulse buyer when it comes to things like furniture and clothing – a fact which drives my bargain-hunting, "compare-all-the-options-first" husband crazy – I had certainly not followed that pattern in my horse shopping. My wake lay littered with dozens of horses rejected on the grounds of being too tall or too small, poor movers, narrow-chested, cow-hocked, sway-backed, too green and skittish, too dull and plain. Two horses I had fallen in love with had failed their pre-purchase vet exams, one with an old tendon injury that had not healed well, the other with early signs of arthritis in her hocks. No wonder, then, that Robert's jaw dropped at those words. All I could do was look at him and shrug my shoulders. Did I know why I was convinced this was the right horse? No. Did I know he WAS right? Without a doubt.

As I did not have my own trailer at this point, I paid one of the owners of Willowbrook to pick Henk up with me. Jack's trailer was one of those large, comfy aluminium four-horse jobs that's the equivalent of a horsey stretch limo. Henk would be comfortable for his first-ever trailer ride, getting the star treatment on the long way home. The trailer could be configured into a loose-box, which worked perfectly for shipping babies who had no experience being tied for long periods of time, if at all.

Still, as the day approached to pick Henk up, I began to worry (something I'm very good at). How would he handle the two-hour ride? We'd be pulling him away from his dam for the first time in his life, herding him onto a strange contraption with wheels, and shaking him up over bumpy country roads. I had visions of a panicked little horse spinning around the box in fear, screaming for his mother, working himself into a sweat or worse, falling and thrashing around on the floor while Jack and I drove on, blissfully unaware. I called Harry and voiced my concerns, leaving out the more dramatic scenarios I had imagined.

"He'll be a lamb," Harry said, sounding one hundred percent

certain and dismissing the idea of weaning the foal a week or so before the ship date. I could sense there would be little point arguing with him.

Henk was wearing a halter when we arrived, but he'd obviously had no training in how to lead. We more or less carried him onto the trailer while one of Harry's helpers led the protesting mare away. She screamed as she entered the barn, and Henk answered with a few baby whinnies of his own. I felt my stomach flipping. Weaning was as traumatic, I thought, for the humans as for the horses. Soon every horse within earshot had joined in the chorus, and it became impossible to distinguish the calls of the separated pair.

We said our "good-byes" and headed out the gate, hoping that once out earshot, the swaying of the trailer would soothe Henk. It often had that effect, lulling a nervous horse as it rocked gently back and forth.

Without a camera in the trailer, it was difficult to guess what was going on in there, particularly with a baby. When a grown horse frets, worries and bangs around, it's not hard to feel the jolts all the way up in the truck, but a foal has no impact on a big trailer. On the other hand, we wanted to give the foal time to settle before stopping to check on him, so we pulled out onto the highway and drove for twenty gut-wrenching minutes before Jack finally pulled over into a service centre. I was out and at the trailer door before the truck had fully stopped, heart beating and palms sweating. What would I find?

I pulled open the top part of the dutch door and peeked in. Henk was standing, splay-legged for balance, in the centre of the stall without a drop of sweat on his black coat or a single hair out of place. He looked at me with an "are we there yet?" expression on his face. I started to laugh as relief flooded me.

"I guess he's OK," I said as Jack stepped up beside me.

We got back in the truck and drove the rest of the way to my house. When we arrived and opened the trailer we found Henk in virtually the same spot as before, but this time he whinnied at us. It was not a panicky, worried scream. It was more of a greeting, as if to say, "Hey, it's you guys again. I wondered where you'd got to…"

Lamb indeed. Just as Harry had predicted.

We let down the trailer ramp, attached a lead rope to his halter, and guided Henk toward the barn. I'd asked the kids to put the other horses in the barn before got home so there wouldn't be any running around and fussing. The barn was located between the two paddocks, and I wanted a nice, quiet reception for the newcomer. We turned Henk loose in his new stall, and he immediately started exploring. Not a shy horse, by any means, he checked out all the new sights and smells, pushing the bedding around with his small black nose. He heard Olivia moving in the next stall and went over to have a look.

Nearly the same age, though Olivia was a good deal taller, I expected they would be paddock buddies and playmates – best friends within the herd. I'd put them side-by-side in the barn to get acquainted. No shrinking violet herself, Olivia decided to come over and see what all the excitement was about in the next stall. What were the humans looking at? Was there not a rule in this barn that she, Olivia, should be the centre of attention? What was going on? She poked her head over the partition to have a look. She caught sight of Henk and flew back across her stall to stand in the corner, shaking and traumatized. It took us a while to stop laughing. Clearly, a pitch-black colt with a spiky Mohawk hairdo was not what she had been expecting to find!

Bemused, Henk stuck his nose through the bars and snorted. Olivia pasted herself more tightly to the wall. He pricked his ears, rubbed his nose up and down the divider, shuffled around a little, tossed his head. He was making it obvious he wanted to meet her, but it would take Olivia quite some time before she ventured all the way over to the partition between their stalls again, still eyeing him suspiciously. Henk was at full attention, head high, ears pricked, flared nostrils breathing in her scent. It occurred to me he had never seen anything but a solid-black horse in his life, and the long-legged, brightly-marked filly must have looked as strange to him as a blond-haired Scandinavian to a villager in the Amazon rainforest.

Eventually they would become friends, of course, and even work out a team approach to handling strange new situations. Henk would be first in, scoping out the lay of the land, while Olivia hung back as his cover. I suppose it seemed only fitting to Olivia that the little black horse should sacrifice himself to protect the Princess, and Henk was OK with that. He had no issues with sticking his velvety nose into everything first. As I would soon discover, exploring the world with his nose would be a lifelong habit with this horse.

Physically the two foals were very different. With a Dutch Warmblood sire and a tall, elegant Thoroughbred dam, Olivia was all legs. When I eventually sold her as a two-year-old, she was still grazing with her front legs splayed out like a giraffe at the watering hole, exerting considerable effort to reach the ground. And those legs were fine and elegant, even with the knobby knees and hocks that would take her years to grow into. She was a brilliant bay with a narrow white blaze that set off her pretty, feminine face. No one mistook Olivia for a colt. She was all girl.

Henk, on the other hand, was compact and upright, with a rounded rump and a neck that seemed stuck onto his shoulders vertically. His head was always held high, his dark eyes perpetually looking for trouble, and usually finding it. Solid black with a fuzzy mane and tail that would eventually grow into the long, wavy tresses that are a Friesian trademark, he looked like nothing so much as a stuffed-toy horse. His legs, while long in the disproportionate way of all foals, were solid and strong and he was amazingly agile. We had installed a drain at one end of the paddock to guide water away to a ditch, and to keep it from eroding I'd lined it with some of the many rocks the big excavator had dug up while grading the sand ring. Although it was just a ditch running through part of the paddock, easy to walk around and with nothing of particular interest on the other side, Henk soon ventured into it, picking his way carefully over the smooth rocks, probably just to show he could.

Henk turned out to be a gregarious soul, bucking the usual horse habit of choosing friends within the herd and sticking with them. Henk could get along with anyone, and often changed grazing,

grooming and fly-swatting partners. Defying the laws of the
herd, he would sometimes share a hay-pile with the alpha horse,
sometimes with the lowest creature on the totem-pole. While the
horses always presented themselves at the gate in a specific order
to come in for dinner, starting with the top horse and finishing
with the most submissive, Henk would never be that predictable. He knew better than to challenge for the top spot, but he
would sometimes come in second, sometimes last. When a new
horse was introduced into the herd, Henk could be counted on
to accept him first, easing the newcomer into the hierarchy.

Herd introductions can be traumatic. Horses have been known
to chase a newcomer mercilessly, sometimes into fences or gates,
sometimes trapping them in a corner and beating them up with
hooves and teeth. My friend Gail spent several panicky hours
once, searching for a friend's mare who'd been left in her care
for a week. Gail's horses had harassed the mare so badly she'd
jumped the fence and taken off down the road.

When Olivia came to live at my barn, the others had seemed to
accept her easily. No one, including Sahara, had paid her much
attention. Then one day North decided he didn't like the filly after all and began to chase her hard. Oscar soon joined in. I tried
to break up the chase, but a two-legged human is helpless against
fleet-footed four-legged horses, even old ones. I'd run around
pointlessly, waving a whip and trying to turn the geldings away
long enough to give Olivia an escape route, but without much
luck. The horses would simply wheel around and fly to the other
side of the paddock, driving the filly before them, while I flapped
my arms and shouted helplessly in their wake. The situation
looked dire until Sahara decided to take charge. I never knew

what prompted her decision, but suddenly she came thundering out of nowhere, cut between the terrified filly and her tormentors, then spun and let fly with both hinds, landing a solid kick in North's midsection. He grunted as her hooves connected with his ribs. He was not seriously hurt, but definitely chastised. With a baleful look backward toward the filly who could finally stop running and stood breathing hard, obviously shaken, he slunk off to stand beneath a tree, nursing his wounded pride. Oscar joined him for moral support, while Olivia and Sahara wandered off to graze together in the adjoining paddock. The geldings never bothered the filly again, and Olivia had found a surrogate mother.

Since I had no intention of letting anything similar happen again, I left Henk in his stall his first full day at out farm while I went to work, planning to turn him out in the afternoon, alone in one paddock, allowing him to meet everyone safely over the fence with me supervising from the sidelines. Needless to say I was a little shaken up when my husband called me on my cell phone as I was driving home from work to tell me that the other horses apparently did not like Henk.

"You put him out with them?" I asked, barely controlling a rising panic.

"Yeah. He looked lonely."

I swallowed, took a deep breath, tried not to imagine a little black foal smashing headlong into a solid oak fence with four large horses hard on his heels, teeth snapping.

"They all chased him. Aren't they usually nice to babies?"

Oh god. "Where is he now?"

"In his stall."

"He let you catch him?" I was finally able to breathe again.

"He came right back to the barn himself."

"Smart baby!"

After that, it did not take long for the little black horse to become part of the herd. After a couple of days alone in the adjoining paddock, I put Olivia out with him, and then The Big Red Mare. Whatever her other faults, Sahara was proving to be good with the babies, and more than capable of keeping the other horses in line. Once she'd accepted Henk, I knew Oscar and North would leave him alone. They knew better than to draw the wrath of Sahara down on their old heads again. Sometimes the old geldings even played with the foals for a while, running and kicking up their heels in a way I had not seen them do in years. Then they would tire of the game and wander off to eat, leaving the youngsters to entertain each other.

Henk had won Oscar and North over, drawing out at least a kind of bemused tolerance from the old ones. But me? He stole my heart.

Never had I met a horse with so much personality (horsenality?). Henk never had a bad day. The moment he saw me – or any human -- his ears pricked way up, their tips nearly touching, and he would trot over to stick his head into my chest, looking for a hug. He would stand contentedly, eyes half-closed, enjoying the physical contact. If I was working in the paddock – mending fences or mucking out manure – he would follow me around like a puppy. This was not always helpful. He would paw at the wheelbarrow until it tipped, steal my pitchfork or hammer if I put them down, or stick his nose between me and the board I was attempting to re-attach. He would rather be with humans than horses. Given the choice, I was sure he'd prefer to live in the house, watching TV with us instead of sleeping in the barn with the other equines. I could picture Henk on a couch – if IKEA made one strong enough to hold him – kicking back with an apple juice and a bowl of popcorn, watching *The Black Stallion* or *Seabiscuit*.

So, naturally, having this young charmer in my life made me want to have another Friesian. After all, Henk was only a baby. It would be years before I would be able to ride him. And besides, if one Friesian was great, how wonderful would two be? The day I saw Wilbert advertised for sale, I knew I'd found my second beautiful black horse.

He was not quite four years old, barely started under saddle, almost 16hh and stunning. Wilby was a classic, Baroque Friesian – all curves – the type you would see pulling a gorgeous carriage or dressed in fancy armour carrying a medieval knight or king into battle. He had the deep, dark, soft eyes that reflect a gentle soul, and the kindest spirit of any horse I have ever had the privilege to ride. He had not been ridden all winter when I went to the breeder's farm to meet him. I would have to ride him in a big open field next to a busy road. Having lately had to deal with spooky, temperamental horses, I asked the breeder how I should expect Wilbert to react: what was he likely to do out there?

"He will be happy," Ted said, and it was clear from the way he answered my question that he thought me a little strange for asking. What was I expecting the horse to do? I could have provided a long list.

Wilbert *was* happy. Attentive but relaxed, forward but careful on the slightly icy footing. Even when a transport truck blew by on the road next to us, Wilbert did nothing more than push up into the bridle a little. His gaits were wonderful, he had a lovely soft mouth that was light in my hands, and he apparently enjoyed his work.

Ted was clearly proud when I told him how much I liked his horse, and that I would like to buy him. But he was a little sad, too.

"It is always hard when you sell the horse," he explained in his heavy Dutch accent. Ted had moved to Canada only recently, and brought a small band of horses, including Wilbert and his stunning dam, with him. Dairy cattle were his business. The horses were an obvious love. "It is hard to see them leave."

He gave me the name of a couple who had bought Wilbert's full brother the year before – in case I wanted references, or just to chat -- and asked if he could come visit Wilbert at our farm sometime in the summer. I had never bought a horse from anyone like this before, and I have often wondered since if Ted's gentle manner and obvious love for his horses is at least partly responsible for Wilbert's sweet nature.

Wilbert was a perfect gentleman on the long trip home to our little farm, and while he had a good, long look at his surroundings when he backed off the trailer, there were no hysterics. He walked calmly into his stall and touched noses with his neighbour through the stall partition. Next morning I gave Wilbert a paddock to himself, allowing him to meet his new barn-mates over the fence. This went well until one of the horses got, I suppose, a little too fresh with him and then Wilbert wheeled around and let fly with both hind feet in the offending horse's direction. A sixteen-foot oak board, nailed to three separate posts along its length, popped off the fence and flew a remarkable distance into the other paddock.

"Wow," we said in unison. Robert, Michael, Christopher and I had all been leaning on a fence, watching to see how the first meeting would go.

"That's impressive," I said.

"You don't wanna be behind him when he does THAT," Michael added.

"Cool," Christopher said.

"I'd better get my hammer," Robert said, climbing through the fence.

Over the next week or so, Wilbert removed several fence-boards this way. He had me patrolling the paddocks, picking up planks before a horse stepped on a nail, wondering how well this powerful horse would fit into the herd. Was he going to maim somebody? And then he stopped kicking. When I gradually introduced the other horses into his paddock, he matter-of-factly took his rightful place as boss, subjugating even the mighty Sahara. But where she had been a tyrannical alpha horse, chasing her lowly subjects away from their hay out of plain orneriness, Wilbert left them alone. Once he established his position, he was happy to let them be. If a horse stepped out of line, a simple pinning of the ears or a nip on the offending horse's butt or shoulder would usually restore order. Thankfully, it was rare to see Wilbert so much as threaten another horse with those awesome hind feet of his.

Being number one came naturally to this beautiful creature, and he carried himself with the air of a born leader. Every stride seemed thought-out, each footfall placed just "so." There was an unhurried dignity to this horse and a calmness. He seemed simply and quietly in control of his world.

I could hardly wait to go riding every day. Having spent the last few years almost exclusively on tall, long, leggy Thoroughbreds and warmbloods, having Wilby's massive shoulders and high, arched neck in front of me was amazing. He was remarkably short-bodied, supple, and light on his feet. Although he'd had very little formal training, he was always responsive to his rider – and happy to do what was asked of him, once he understood it. Within a few months of beginning his training, I found he was so "tuned in" that virtually all I had to do was to THINK "canter," and off we would go. And what a canter it was! Big and bouncy and incredibly powerful, it was impressive to watch and fun to ride.

Wilby, as I had come to call him once his personality revealed it-self and the registered name began to sound too stiff and formal for him, would try anything I asked him to, although he would not always be successful at it. Trotting over poles was more like the lumberjack sport of log-rolling at first, as Wilby would trip over or step on every single pole even while gamely picking his feet up high and trying to aim for the spaces in-between. No matter how I adjusted the spacing, the poles never seemed to be in the right place until, one day, he "got it," and began to negotiate them with considerable style.

When I eventually asked him to jump over a small obstacle, he trotted up to it uncertainly, hoping until the very last moment that I would change my mind, then launched himself over in a resigned sort of way. It came a little more easily on the second and third try, but when I dismounted after that particular lesson he fixed me with a look that seemed to say "Look, lady, I was bred to pull carriages and carry people around on Sunday outings to the park and look magnificent doing it. Nowhere in my pedigree does it say anything about jumping!"

Because of his high head carriage, massive build and solid black colour, Wilby is an imposing presence. The first time Ed walked into his stall to administer annual vaccines, he took a step back as Wilby turned toward him.

"Wow," he said. "He's huge!"

I had to convince him that the Friesian was, in fact, only 16 hands tall – quite average for a riding horse.

I have come to wonder if the black colour and imposing presence were bred into the Friesian specifically for his original role of warhorse, for purposes of intimidation. After all, the basis of classical dressage were movements developed for warfare. The high-stepping piaffe (trot in place) and the floaty passage are both awe-inspiring gaits that would humble a mere foot soldier. The "airs above the ground," still performed by the Lipizzan stallions of the Spanish Riding School, include the Levade, a half-rear that protects the rider from sword and spear, the Capriole, a leap straight up into the air followed by a powerful backward kick with both hind feet, and the Courbette, a full rear followed by several hops forward on the hind legs. Intimidating indeed. Besides the strength to carry a knight in full armour, could the build and presence of the Friesian not have been intended for a similar purpose?

Indeed, when I eventually began to use Wilby in my therapeutic riding program years later, several of his riders would be intimidated at first. Like Becky, a young woman who badly wanted to ride, but who was prone to anxiety attacks and proved to be very nervous around horses. I started her out on Oscar. Although he stands 17 hands high, Oscar has become a peaceful old soul with a gentle manner, his spookiness all gone, and quite unintimidating because of his head-down, mosey-along attitude. He tends to be my first choice for nervous riders, and he was the horse I chose for Becky. She was happy enough at first, but found Oscar's fidgeting when asked to stand still for long periods of time disconcerting. Becky needed an occasional long halt to compose herself and deal with rising panic, and Oscar would begin to fret. I eventually decided to make the switch to Wilby. Becky nearly refused to make the change. She found Wilby overwhelming. I suggested she try him, and if she hated it, we would put her right back on Oscar. Once mounted and swaying along in that wonderfully smooth, rhythmical walk, Becky began to smile. Then she discovered how happy Wilby was to stand stock still for as long as she liked, and how he welcomed her when she approached him before her lesson, head down and eyes soft, and nothing could have convinced her to go back.

Among the volunteers he quickly became a favourite, with the chance to "warm up Wilby" with a quick ride before a lesson becoming a treat many looked forward to all week. He would patiently take each rider around, letting the volunteers have some fun before the work of the therapeutic lesson began.

All this is not to say, however, that Wilby was the perfect ride right from the start. I tend to forget now, five years on, that our first summer together had some frustrations. As with many young horses, Wilby had one canter lead he did not like, and when he did strike out correctly he was so stiff and bent in the wrong direction that my saddle tended to slip on his very round frame. Eventually he would learn to bend and yield his ribcage in both directions, but not until we had ridden many, many circles, serpentines, figure-eights and leg yields.

He also required schooling at the mounting block. Walking off (or worse) is a habit I detest, having once been dragged with one foot in the stirrup when a horse, took off as I was half-way up. I'd lost my grip and fallen. With a foot snagged in the stirrup and dragging behind an increasingly panicky horse who couldn't understand what I was doing down there, I'd felt helpless. No way to stop him, no way to reach up and get my foot free, I was lucky to come loose before anything really awful happened. The experience taught me to insist on perfect manners during the mount, and Wilby came without those. A few sessions at the mounting block, simply insisting on good behaviour, and waiting him out until he stood stock still, did the trick.

The only other major obstacle turned out to be teaching Wilby to work "long and low," head stretched down and neck extended, relaxing the muscles of his back. This is a useful exercise for any horse, but comes only with difficulty to the high-headed Friesian. Eventually, though, Wilby did learn to lower his head when asked, both under saddle and when having his bridle or halter put on.

In all my work with Wilby, and eventually with Henk, I have been struck by the Friesians' intelligence. What most horses will master only after many, many repetitions, the Friesian tends to pick up after only a few lessons, and the lessons stick. If my two are typical examples of the breed, then the Friesian is a trainer's dream.

Maybe that trainability, combined with their stunning looks, is the reason Friesians appear in so many movies. In *Alexander*, *300*, *Ladyhawke*, *Eragon*, *The Mask of Zorro* (a clipped Friesian playing an Andalusian), *Interview with the Vampire*, *The Chronicles of Narnia*, plus virtually every period piece that has a fancy carriage in it, Friesians play minor and major roles on the silver screen. To me, they embody all the things that have attracted humans to horses throughout our long history together and inspired artists from the earliest cavemen to da Vinci and beyond. In my life, at least, they have come to represent the best of what humans and horses have shared since human first sat on the back of a horse.

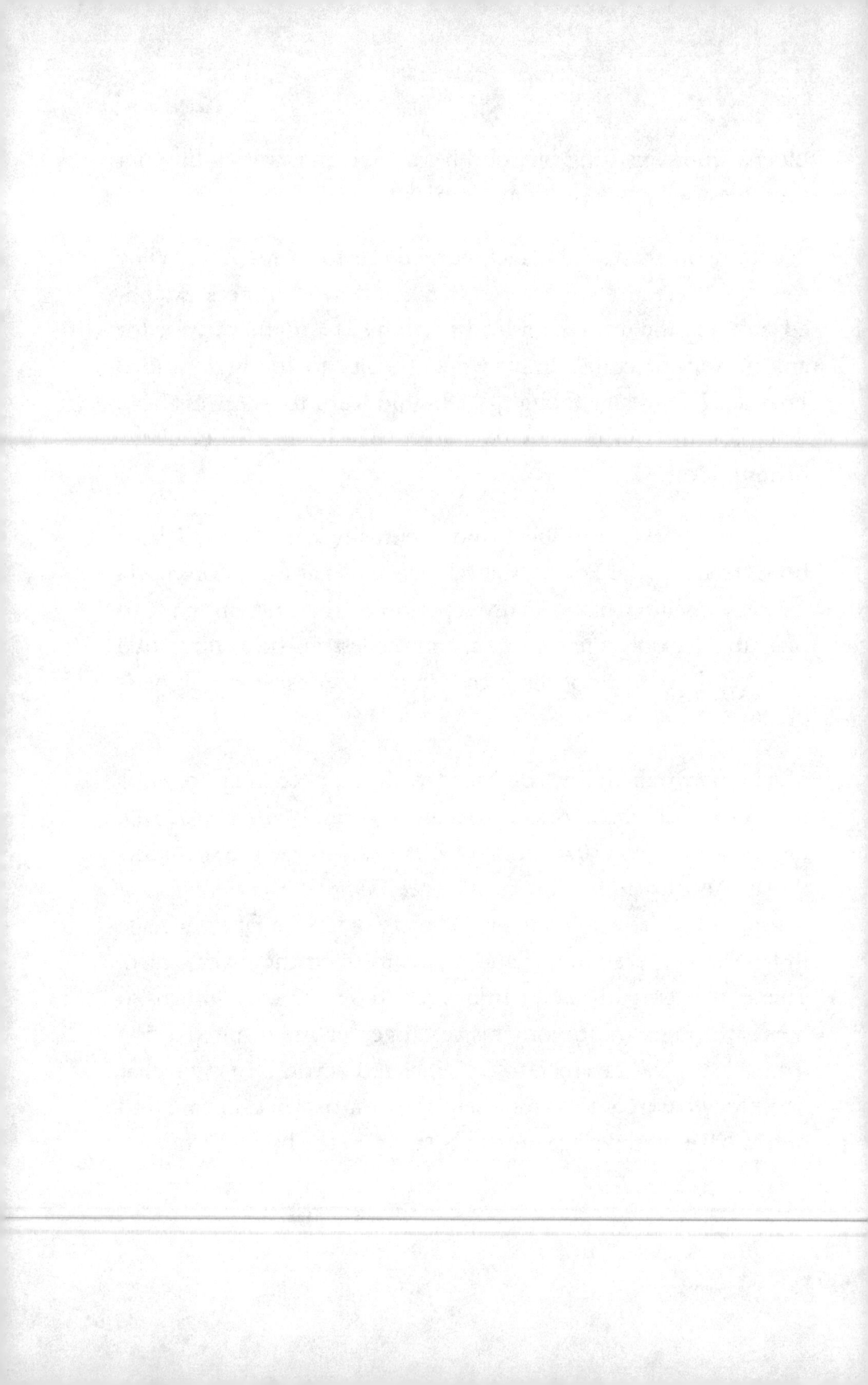

5

The greatness of a nation and its moral prog-
ress can be judged by the way its animals are
treated. I hold that, the more helpless a crea-
ture, the more entitled it is to protection by
man from the cruelty of man.
(Mahatma Ghandi)

If the Friesians represented the best of the horse-human relationship, our next three horses represented some of the worst.

Rosie, Ronan and Moose came to us starving and sick, the neglected, unwanted by-products of an industry that treats horses
as ledger-entries in a corporation's books rather than the living,
breathing, feeling creatures that they are.

Whether they end up on someone's dinner plate or in a bowl of
dog food, discarded from a racing stable, tied to a carousel giving pony rides in the hot sun, neglected in an overgrazed pasture
without shelter, or rented out and given only the minimum care
to keep them alive, some horses are just plain unlucky.

Our three were headed for slaughter as weanlings – products of the PMU industry which provides the raw material – the urine of pregnant mares – for the production of hormones used by thousands of women to control the symptoms of menopause.

Like many people I knew, I had given this concept very little thought when I'd first heard about PMU hormones as an effective treatment. "Cool," I probably thought at the time. "Horses are helping people once again." I had not stopped to consider just how this urine would be obtained from the mares; that it would not magically appear in the laboratories of the pharmaceutical companies that made the drugs.

Just how DO you obtain vast quantities of pregnant mare urine?

You do it by paying ranchers to keep herds of mares pregnant. You do it by tying the mares in small standing-stalls so the harnesses and receptacles that collect the urine can stay in place. Twenty-four hours a day. You do it by producing tens of thousands of foals that are in the end nothing but a byproduct of your business. Surplus. Unwanted. Fodder for the slaughter-houses. You do it by valuing a woman's relief from the occasional hot-flash more highly than the life of a horse. You do it by not giving a damn.

Thankfully, though, a few people did give a damn. They took the time to find out, and got angry. They wrote letters and articles and got the word out. They took or bought the foals when they were weaned and tried to find them decent homes. They talked to the ranchers and convinced a few to give at least some thought to what they were breeding so the foals would be a little better quality and easier to place as riding horses. None of this helped the mares much, but it did save some of the foals. A few ranchers listened, and ended up producing decent stock that found willing takers. Many, though, continued to breed anything that moved, and evidently had no qualms about sending the foals to be slaughtered for meat.

In the end the thing that ended most of this misery was a link between hormone replacement therapy and cancer. Suddenly demand for the treatment dried up. Now the problem was to try to save the mares. Thousands of these mares had never been ridden and were now too old to train. They had spent their entire lives producing babies and commercial urine, and nothing more. Now the organizations that had tried to find homes for the babies were trying to find homes for the mothers, too. It was a mostly hopeless task.

Our foals came from a local farmer who had bought several hundred weanlings from a ranch in Manitoba and brought them to his farm, about 50 km from our place. He would sell what he could, and "ship" the rest ("ship" is the euphemism many people in the horse industry use when they mean "send to slaughter." It sounds less awful, but the end is just the same).

I saw his ad in the local classifieds, offering weanlings for sale, and I tried hard to ignore it. Robert was all enthusiasm. Many of these foals were draft-crosses, and he wanted a big horse that he could eventually ride. And they were cheap. Besides, giving one a good home would be a nice thing to do. It made sense, but I didn't want any part of it. How could you ever choose one, I wondered, knowing what would happen to the many others that stayed? How could you look at so many lives you knew would soon come to a horrible end? How could you keep those eyes and faces out of your dreams? How could you point to one, and say, "yes, that one can live," and ignore the scores of others?

I didn't want to go, so Robert went to see them alone, and then he brought home the stories: of the Belgian-cross colt with the big Roman nose; the little black colt with the four white stockings and big white blaze who was always hiding in a little knot of friends; of the muck and dirt they lived in.

He knew precisely what he was doing. Eventually I went with him, because the stories had made the horses real, and now I could no longer leave them there. I even made the kids come along – not to make them feel bad, but to see what we as a species were capable of doing to the creatures who share our world. It was not a pleasant sight. There were so many foals, milling around, trying to get a bite of hay from the big round bales that were being dominated by the biggest and strongest. Most were sick and skinny and scared. Those that could run away from us did so, eyeing any human warily and wondering what nastiness awaited them next. Some could not run. They were too sick or injured to walk or even to get up off the ground. They lay in cold mud and waited to die.

"You don't get to pick at those ranches," the farmer explained. "You take whatever they herd onto the trailer. The good with the bad."

There was no question of the farmer offering them veterinary care. That would easily wipe out his entire profit from the venture, and profit was what he was after. He made no secret of the final destination of any colts that remained unsold after a month. They would be heading to a slaughter-house in Montreal.

"I worked on one of those ranches once," a fellow buyer offered as we walked among the babies. From the look of him he was an old-time horseman with an eye for a good horse and no patience for sentimentality. "In those days they didn't bother to try and sell 'em," he said. "We'd let the mares foal out, then hit the foals over the head and throw them in a heap. They weren't worth nothin'."

Evidently, from the look of these sorry little creatures, and the number still left unclaimed after three weeks of advertising, they still were not worth much, in most people's opinions.

We came back a few days later with our trailer. We took the Roman-nosed Belgian and the black colt. Robert had already picked them out and Christopher and Michael loved them. I didn't have to choose. The black colt had a friend – another small black horse that seemed even more shy and scared than he was. It was a very ordinary colt and we left it behind. But then there was the filly. Big and brash and pushy, with strange rose-grey colouring. Something about her appealed to me. I tried to ignore her, but somehow I kept noticing her. She bossed the other foals around. Pushed her way to the hay-bale. Led the charge when they bolted away from us.

"Let's take that one, too," I said.

Robert looked at me and laughed.

"In for a penny, in for a pound," I said. "What's one more?"

So the filly came and more than a hundred others stayed. I try not to think about them. The other day Christopher remembered Ronan's little black buddy.

"We should have taken him, too," he said, and he was right. I try not to consider what might have happened to the little colt.

So they came home. The Belgian, Moose, the black colt, Ronan, and the weird grey filly, named Rosie for her pinkish colour. We filled the front of our trailer with hay-bales to keep the foals away from the escape doors on the trip home and chased the three of them onto the trailer. It took some work, cutting them from the herd and shooing them onto the trailer where they barely fit, wedged in side-by-side. It was a tight fit and it kept them from getting knocked around on the trip back to our place. We had a camera in the trailer and watched the babies on a TV screen in the truck. They spent the whole trip with their faces in the hay bales, eating.

It was only once we got them home and were able to see them close up that we realized just how skinny they were – hip-bones poking out and every rib visible under the matted winter coats. Moose's head looked three sizes too big for his wasted body.

"Don't get too attached to them," I warned the kids pointlessly. "They might not make it."

"What do you mean?" Michael asked.

"I mean some of them die. They're too sick or too malnourished

I know someone who got one last year and it only lasted a week. So don't get too attached."

Right.

We put them in quarantine with lots of hay and a run-in shelter of their own. At least they would not have to fight for food or a place to get out of the cold autumn rain now. They didn't appreciate these luxuries immediately, though. They were in a strange place once again, and this time the security of their herd was gone. They were very scared.

We guesstimated their age at four months or so, and in that time their experience of humans had been anything but pleasant. Born in a pasture somewhere in Manitoba, they were left in relative peace for a few months with their dams. While no care of any sort would be offered, they were also left alone. The mares would be re-bred, and once it was time to bring them back in to begin the urine harvest once again, the foals would be sent on their way. In the case of our three, that meant a long ride on a crowded trailer all the way to Ontario. At no point had anyone made any attempt to befriend or gentle them. They were wild as hares.

This proved to be an issue when we tried to treat the ringworm they were all infested with. Ronan was the worst. Most of the hair on his face was gone and the skin had a raw, irritated look. He was always scratching his head on the fenceposts, the walls of the run-in shelter, the other two foals. Moose and Rosie looked less pitiful, but both had round bald patches of their own. When they eventually recovered and the hair grew back, Rosie's would grow in white where the ring-worm had been, giving her strange-looking dapples in places where dapples don't usually appear. She looked so odd that the vet took a picture for his records.

We tried to treat the ring-worm with ointments and sprays, but the foals wanted nothing to do with that. We also needed to de-worm them, but that would require capturing the young beasts and putting halters on them, then squirting de-worming paste into their mouths. No easy feat. We lured them into the run-in shelter, blocked their exit with a kind of portable stock device, and tried to convince them to let us slip the halters on their heads. After repeated breaks for freedom – always led by Rosie -- and much exasperation on our part, Moose and Rosie eventually yielded. Ronan, however, would not. He became expert at hiding behind the filly, ducking his head just out of reach. The filly was a willing accomplice, blocking our access to "her" baby. It was an exercise in frustration and futility that lasted many days. When Ronan finally succumbed and darted from the run-in wearing a brand new bright blue halter, we felt as proud as if we had just trained a Kentucky Derby winner (though nowhere near as rich). The de-worming was even more amusing. Robert and I ended up wearing more de-worming paste than we were able to get into the foals. Michael and Christopher sat on the fence laughing. But at last, the foals were on their way to better health.

"Taming" the foals would have been much easier if we could have bribed them with treats. Often, horses are much more willing to negotiate putting up with a new experience (a halter, saddle, the first time having their feet trimmed etc.) if they receive a carrot or piece of apple as a reward. But these horses were unbribeable!

Never having experienced food other than grass or hay, they refused to eat anything else. We tried apples and carrots -- sliced,
cubed, grated, mixed with molasses and without; we tried sugar
cubes and mints; we tried commercial horse treats and home-
made concoctions, sweet feed, pellets and oats; nothing worked.
The foals would sniff whatever was on offer in the buckets that
day, push the morsels around with their noses, lip them a little,
then walk away.

At first, their refusal to eat anything but hay only meant they'd
taken longer to fattern up, and that food would not be helpful in
their early training. But once Rosie came down with Strangles,
getting food into her became a priority.

Strangles. The word made me go cold. I knew she had it before
our vet Ed confirmed it. The sores weeping pus under her jaw
were unmistakable. I felt sick to my stomach. Strangles. A nasty,
highly contagious respiratory infection, Strangles had been all
but wiped out through careful management and vaccinations in
our part of the country until people started bringing in PMU
foals.

"Think of them as four-legged Petrie dishes," Ed had warned
me when I'd called him the week before we picked our three
babies up. "They've never been vaccinated against anything, and
neither have most of their mothers, so the foals get no immunity
from them through their milk like other horses do. I can't tell
you how many times I've seen people bring one of these foals
home, and within a week every horse in their barn is snot-nosed
and coughing. Or worse."

"So how do I keep my other horses safe?"

"The best way? Don't get the foals. But it's too late for that, isn't it?" he said with a tone of resignation in his voice. Vets, more than anyone, know that most horse people are sorely lacking in horse sense.

"Kinda, yeah."

"OK, then. Quarantine. Keep them completely separate from the rest of the herd. Change your clothes, change your boots, wash your hands, don't use the same buckets to feed or water them." He was rhyming off his list as I madly wrote instructions down. Good thing we'd already built them their own pen and run-in shelter, I thought.

It was a lot of work and sometimes seemed excessive. I knew other people who had brought home PMUs and had no problems. Changing boots and cover-alls, scrubbing hands – it was a pain in the neck. Once Rosie became sick, though, it all became worthwhile. No one else came down with Strangles in our barn. Ronan and Moose must have already gone through it before we brought them home, so they had immunity, and the others had been vaccinated. That, and the quarantine, had evidently kept them safe.

But Rosie was sick. A cold rain fell hard the day Ed came to see her and the filly stood plastered against the fence as far from us as she could get, head down, pus matting the hair at her throat, water dripping down her flanks. She was the picture of misery.

"What can I do for her?"

"Get her to eat. Try to keep her warm. We could give her Penicillin but I don't recommend it. All it does is drive the infection into a kind of dormancy that can flare up later and be far worse than the original illness. It's best to let it run its course."

Simple advice, to keep her warm and make her eat, but a blanket was out of the question for a horse who had just barely learned to tolerate a halter, and she was too infectious to bring into the barn. So we put her hay into the run-in to encourage her to stay there. The other thing she needed in her starved condition was decent feed to supplement the hay. But she wouldn't eat it. I could not think of a single trick we hadn't tried yet to introduce these creatures to more nutritious feed.

"I think the problem is," I said as we stood around the pen contemplating our little skeletons, "that they don't understand about chewing grain or pellets or carrots. They want it, but when they get it in their mouth, they spit it out again. I think it feels strange to them."

"Why don't we sprinkle some of the pellets on their hay?" Michael suggested. "Maybe they'll accidentally eat some and find out it's good."

"I don't know. It'll just get wasted," I argued.

"No, let's try it," Christopher said in an unusual display of fraternal solidarity. "I think it's a good idea."

And it was. It worked. The foals would pick up a few pellets with their hay and chew everything up together, eventually developing a taste for the stuff. After weeks of trying, sweet victory. Before long the foals were whinnying for their supper and chasing each other from the feed buckets to get more than their fair share. Once Rosie fought off the Strangles infection she, of course, dominated the feed buckets, pinning her ears and snapping at the colts' flanks. Moose and Ronan learned to speed-eat in an effort to keep her from stealing their food. Soon the little bone-racks were covered with layers of muscle and fat, and their over-all health began to improve.

While getting them healthy had been our first priority, we also wanted to start handling the foals and turning them into regular horses who would some day have a job of some description. But they were wild. Naturally suspicious of humans. They had no interest in co-operating with us, but ran as soon as we approached them. Happy to accept food now, they still had no intention of accepting *us*. In this, their ring-worm turned out to be our ally.

The disease had made them itchy. I would often see them scratching on fences and grooming each other. I had a rare brain-storm. I took a plastic curry-comb, the kind with many little hard teeth, and climbed into their pen. While Moose, the quietest of the three, was eating hay, I sidled up to him non-chalantly and gently rubbed his shoulder with the curry-comb the way another horse would "groom" him with its teeth. He considered running away, lifting his head in alarm and tensing his muscles, but what I was doing apparently felt good, the hay was definitely tasty, and so he stood still and continued chewing. I groomed him for a few minutes and left before he became too nervous. Next day I did a little more, and each day after that, always extending the time a little and venturing to other parts of his body with my curry comb. When Rosie came over to see what I was doing I used my other hand to start grooming her, while still focusing on Moose. She did not feel threatened and did not run. Even Ronan was eventually won over, and Robert and the kids would join me, quietly grooming, while the foals discovered that physical contact with humans could actually feel pretty good.

Things progressed quickly from there. Fatter, healthier, and developing a shine to their coats and eyes, the foals began to resemble regular horses instead of something the SPCA would want to take away. We were able to vaccinate them, and began to teach them about picking up their feet so the farrier could trim them.

Naturally Ronan resisted the longest. Having a leg immobilized made him feel vulnerable, I guessed, and we had to progress very slowly to avoid panicking him and losing his hard-won trust. For some reason known only to him, he decided that his left hind was his most important leg, and he would not give it up, tensing up and backing away from any attempt to lift that particular foot. I decided not to force him, but to take my time. The slaughter-house three would be living in the big barn with the others, their quarantine over, before he finally let me pick that foot up without worrying. For weeks, when I came in from doing night chores which included picking out the feet of our seven horses, Robert would ask "how many feet?" And I would report: "twenty-seven." The day I could finally report that all twenty-eight hooves had been successfully picked out felt like a huge victory.

6

Our greatest glory is not in never falling,
but in getting up every time we do.
(Confucius)

At the same time as our three starving foals were learning about life on a small Ontario hobby farm, I was learning about working with special-needs children, volunteering in therapeutic riding programs. Some of the things I learned probably surprised me as much as the taste of grain in their mouths and the feel of a curry-comb in their matted coats surprised the foals.

One of the things I discovered was that I was far happier working in a small, intimate program like Elaine's rather than a large, highly structured one.

Run with rented horses with only Elaine, her partner Debbie, and a handful of volunteers, this incredible program took on some of the most challenging (and challenged) riders I was ever to see in my work. Elaine should have been writing instructor manuals and teaching workshops, she was that good. And passionate. If I hadn't been "sold" on therapeutic riding before, Elaine would have sold me. Even before I saw the results she was able to obtain with her young clients. Her skills were impressive and her enthusiasm was contagious.

Because many of her riders were severely disabled, Elaine worked with one rider at a time. No group lessons at this facility. With the help of two or three volunteers and a succession of horses, Elaine would do five or six lessons a day, two days a week. The rest of the time she had a "real" job to pay the bills (another of the lessons I was learning was that therapeutic riding was not going to make me money!). I volunteered one day a week, and by the time we finished with our last rider, groomed and put away the last horse, packed up the gear and got in our cars to go home, I could barely move. The exhaustion was worse if I was sidewalking rather than leading, since many of Elaine's clients needed constant physical support to stay upright and on the horse. I would be holding the loop on a safety belt and keeping the rider steady for an hour at a time, hour after hour. Thankfully, the horses Elaine leased for her program were all short, so at least my shoulder wasn't dislocated from trying to reach up to a 16- or 17-hand horse's back.

Some of Elaine's riders were so severely disabled, that I wondered if they even knew they were sitting on a horse. These children were non-responsive, shut away in a world of their own that seemed to have very little to do with ours. They would certainly benefit physically from their time spent riding – the movement of the horse would help their joints and muscles even if they did nothing to help the process. But their parents and support workers often said that they detected more than that – behaviour changes too subtle for me to see that told them their children not only knew what was going on, but enjoyed it, too.

Elaine and her physiotherapist partner Debbie impressed me. The children could break your heart. But it was the parents of the riders in this particular program who I found astonishing. Most of them were raising children who would never be able to take care of themselves, living with the knowledge that the only thing standing between their children and an institution was them. They ferried their youngsters from one school, therapeutic facility and specialist to another. They were on-call day and night, with limited respite when a support worker came to take over for a while. They did whatever had to be done, and in the little down time they had in between tasks they always seemed to be combing through the latest research, hoping to find a new therapy, drug or treatment that might offer a hint of improvement in their child's health and quality of life. That was how most of them had found out about therapeutic riding – they would read about it on the Internet or hear something from another parent. The informal networks among the parents of children with special needs, I would come to learn, were powerful. Once one parent found you, others would soon come knocking on the barn door.

Many of Elaine's client families had more than one child, and the siblings sometimes came along to the riding lessons. I could see the parent struggling to give equal time… sufficient time… any time… to the other children. To not let the needs of one child dominate the less obvious but no less real needs of the others.

Others only had one child, and their worlds seemed entirely defined by the tasks of caring for that child. Lindsay was one of those. A young woman who would not look out of place shopping in exclusive Yorkville or "doing lunch" with friends at a trendy bistro, she reminded me of Linda Hamilton in her *Terminator* phase: short, blond, fit and full of energy. But instead of spending her days at a fitness club, Lindsay instead dedicated her waking hours to her son, Nathan. Nathan would never learn to walk or talk or even sit up in a chair without assistance. I never heard him make a sound, and the expression on his face never seemed to change. His eyes were dark and deep but expressed no emotion. Lindsay would carry him into the stable every week, and instead of taking the hour off while he was riding to sit in the sun and read a book or listen to music, she would sidewalk with Nathan, encouraging him with her words and touch. Once, after a lesson, when she took him in her arms to carry him back to her car he reached up and put his arms around her neck. The expression that little gesture brought to her face was so heart-wrenching that I had to look away.

On my hour-long drive home after a day of volunteering I would often think about those parents. Lindsay most of all. Could I do what she was doing? I would ask myself. Would I have the courage? The physical stamina? The strength of character? Or would I crumble? Would I collapse under the weight of self-pity and hopelessness? Could I face the knowledge that once my husband and I were gone, my child would end up in an institution? What did it feel like to forge on, ever optimistic that what you were doing was making some kind of difference, even when there was so little evidence of change?

But it wasn't just the parents who were strong. If some of the riders seemed to have no real understanding of their disability or the possibility of ever leading a different life, others knew exactly. None of them more so than Nikky. Of all of Elaine's clients, she was the one who touched me most deeply, though she was barely disabled at all. Yet. She was a lovely young woman of sixteen who had been diagnosed with Friedreich's Ataxia – if diagnosis was the right word. This degenerative disease would eventually take away her ability to walk and talk, and likely end her life many years too soon. It seemed more like a cruelly punishing sentence, especially for one so young. While Nikky's only symptoms when she came to Elaine's program were an unco-ordinated, jerky way of walking and a slight loss of balance, by the time Elaine closed down her program a year later, Nikky had little feeling in her feet, her balance problems were severe, and she tired easily. These symptoms would continue to get worse until she was confined to a wheel chair with her ability to move and to communicate severely compromised. There was no cure.

I wondered what it would be like for a sixteen-year-old to wake up every morning and face the knowledge of what lay ahead: that every day would bring a little less mastery over her own body and a little more pain. When I was sixteen, I was invincible, able to do anything, growing more powerful each day. I faced a future full of possibility with potential that seemed unlimited. Having that suddenly reversed by some illness I had never heard of would have been unimaginable, and unimaginably cruel.

Nikky's doctors hoped that riding would be able to slow the progress of her physical symptoms, and she told us that she felt more balanced and in control on the horse than on the ground. Equally important, the riding helped to take her mind off things for a little while. She loved the horses, and smiled a lot while in the saddle. That in itself was an accomplishment, I thought.

I'd hoped that Nikky would come and ride at my farm once I had my program set up, since she lived relatively close, but it never happened. Perhaps the passage of time was just too great. I could only imagine what Nikky's life might have been like by the time we were moved in, set up and ready to go at our farm.

One rider who did continue with me was young Lauren. Like Nikky, she and her mom lived north of Toronto, so the drive to my farm would be manageable, while the rest of Elaine's clients lived in the city – a good two hours from my farm. Lauren's disability was relatively mild – she'd had a stroke as an infant, and the left side of her body remained weaker and more difficult for her to control than her right, but she was a bright young woman who'd been riding since the age of three and looked terrific on a horse, with a good solid seat and very good form. Elaine had her riding a steady old horse, and Lauren eventually progressed to being able to ride without a leader – first on a lunge line, the horse working in circles around Elaine while Lauren learned to use her reins for steering and *not* to balance herself in the saddle, then eventually on her own, while Elaine and I stayed nearby in case she needed help.

By the time she'd come to ride with me and had a year on Oscar under her belt, Lauren was able to do a simple dressage test at the walk and trot, and control her horse well enough that we could focus on the finer points, like riding nice round circles and clean transitions from one gait to another. When the weather was warm I'd saddle Henk up for myself and Oscar for Lauren, and we would ride outside in the grassy paddock, enjoying the lovely summer evenings. Lauren was nervous at first. She had gone riding at a friend's farm and had a horse take off with her.

It had been a terrifying experience that she was not anxious to repeat. I knew she could control Oscar, but I kept him on a lead rope the first few times, where he would walk and trot beside Henk, resentful of being held on a rope and taking the occasional nip at my knee in protest. Lauren thought this was hilarious, and it helped take the edge off her fear. After a few times on the lead, she sucked up her courage and asked me to turn her loose. We never went back to the lead rope after that.

I learned so much from Elaine and had such a wonderful time working with her that the news that she would be closing down her program was a major disappointment. She and her husband had bought a farm some years before, and now that he'd retired the time had come, she said, for them to rebuild the house on that farm and go live in it full-time. For the first time in her life, Elaine would be able to have her horses with her at home, and enjoy the life she had always wanted. Unfortunately, the farm was too far away for her to continue working with her current clients. She hoped some day to find a way to do some therapeutic riding again, but only time would tell. In the meantime, she was trying to find programs where her clients could continue to ride, but it was a sad day when we all said good-bye.

I would continue volunteering, moving to one of the largest programs in the Toronto area where I could work with an instructor Elaine knew. This program was impressive, with many horses, instructors, assistants, co-ordinators, and a massive roster of volunteers. Of necessity, the rules were strict here, and the interaction with clients much less personal. I never met most of the parents at all. By virtue of its size, this program was able to serve hundreds of riders every year. They had some wonderful horses and dedicated humans, but I missed the family atmosphere of Elaine's program. After a year or so, I gave up the three-hour round-trip drive and looked for something closer to home.

What I found was an amazing program run by Sue Mott, one of Canada's top competitors in the very demanding sport of combined driving which demands the careful training and precision demonstrated by negotiating intricate patterns in the ring and the bravery (on the part of horse AND driver) to gallop flat-out over a cross-country course full of obstacles and hazards. Every Wednesday night, Sue and an impressively large team of volunteers would offer a group of special-needs kids and adults the opportunity to come out and drive Sue's Welsh ponies and one large, sweet, Percheron mare. The advantage to driving is that you can give the student "control" of the horse or pony with a set of reins that clip to the reins held by the teacher sitting beside him in the cart. The student can do all the steering, but the experienced driver can take over in a heartbeat should she need to. Sue's clients had an absolutely wonderful time driving the ponies around a large grass ring in summer and in the arena once the snow fell, even negotiating obstacle courses marked by traffic pylons. The ponies and carts were lovely. The mood was always fun. I knew I was in the right place the very first night of my very first session when I saw a tiny woman, probably in her forties and exhibiting the physical characteristics of Down Syndrome, come running across the field to where Sue was standing and give her a massive bear-hug. Sue hugged back with enthusiasm.

Since I knew next to nothing about driving, I worked as a "header," holding the pony steady whenever driver and student came to a halt. I also groomed and helped to get the ponies ready, so I eventually figured out all the pieces of harness and how to hitch them to the cart. After the therapeutic lessons were done, Sue would let me take one of the ponies for a drive, and I ended up taking some lessons from her. Driving well is much more difficult than it looks, and maybe more so for a rider who is used to having the horse right there, between her hands and legs. Our straight lines were serpentines, and our circles were never quite round, although the pony I was driving could do such elementary figures in his sleep. He was an accomplished show pony who even competed with some of Sue's disabled drivers at the reins. And won! What a wonderful feeling for the youngster who could, probably for the first time in her life, compete on equal footing with everyone else, and win.

The gentleman who drove the Percheron was an artist in the driver's seat. You would swear that horse could read his mind. And he was amazing to watch with the clients, too. Gruff, no-nonsense and all business, he specialized in working with the students who were prone to tuning out or shutting down. He could cajole the most pouty of teens out of his mood and have him working the reins and clucking away to that big gray mare in no time.

I would come to discover once I had my own program up and running, that coaxing youngsters into co-operating would be one of the challenges, particularly with children who are autistic or suffer from fetal alcohol syndrome. They can be much more moody than your average teen, and when they decide they've had enough of something, then they have had "ENOUGH, thank you very much, get me off this horse right now or I'll just sit here with my arms crossed and refuse to move, or I may start yelling, too."

Although I'm getting better, I still occasionally make the mistake of asking a rider for just one too many repetitions of an exercise I'm using to teach a skill like steering (using their reins to guide a horse through a row of pylons, for example), and then that stony look will come over her face, or he will drop the reins in a huff, and I know I've gone on too long. It's then I think back to that most skillful of drivers in Sue's programs and use some of his tricks to get that lost co-operation back. Still, it's best not to let it happen in the first place. In this, as in so many things, the experience I had with Sue and Elaine has served as both guidance and inspiration. I still look back at those two programs as some of the most rewarding time I've spent around horses. The camaraderie, the teamwork, the skill and unbounded generosity of the two instructors made it a pleasure to volunteer my time.

And like frightened little Ronan, afraid of his own shadow for so long but finding a way to become more trusting ever so slowly, everyone blossomed in the caring atmosphere of those stables and riding arenas – clients and volunteers alike.

7

*Never approach a bull from the front, a horse
from the rear, or a fool from any direction.*
(Unknown)

While it was never clear to me why Ronan felt more protective of
his left hind than any of his other three legs, I did understand his
fear of surrendering a foot to me. A horse's primary defense from
danger is to run away, and he cannot do that if his leg is immobilized. And Ronan's first few months of life had given him plenty
of reasons not to trust humans, so letting me lift and hold his
foot would be an act of faith – that much harder since Ronan was
a born pessimist. He expected the worst possible outcome from
every new situation he encountered – wearing a halter, standing
in cross-ties, having his teeth checked or vaccines administered.
Even moving from the temporary run-in shed and paddock to
the barn had been traumatic for him. Like a child who's had a
bad start in life, Ronan found it difficult to trust.

Sahara had no such excuses. This mare had received nothing but
the finest care since the day she was born, along with excellent –
if limited – training. So the first time she had reared while under

saddle – soon after I'd bought her and was still boarding her at Willowbrook – I had been shocked. Rearing was not a vice I was prepared to tolerate. I've never minded a buck or two if a horse is feeling feisty, or a spook-and-run if a deer happens to pop out of the woods during a trail ride, but rearing is a nasty bit of business – often more a sign of willfulness than fear – and can result in the horse flipping over backward and landing on its rider. I had no intention of ending up underneath twelve hundred pounds of horse.

Fortunately, I had planned to lunge Sahara before riding her that day. She was still new to the farm then, and to the arena with its unique wind-noises and scary corners, and she and I were new to each other. Ten minutes or so on the lunge line would settle her down before I got on her back for my lesson with the barn coach, Karla. I was about to attach the sidereins to Sahara's bit when she went up without warning, and I was left looking at her belly. It's shocking how tall a horse is when she stands straight up on her hind legs right in front of you. Sahara was a pillar of red towering over me.

And then she fell. She crashed backward into the arena dirt onto my beautiful new saddle. It was spectacular. A mighty "thump," legs waving in the air as she struggled to roll over onto her belly, and then she was on her feet in a heart-beat, shaking the sand out of her mane and looking startled. I moved toward her automatically, checking her over for injuries, but I felt a little dazed. What had just happened? Fortunately she was unharmed and even my saddle had escaped with only a few minor scratches, but why had she reared up like that? There had been nothing to frighten her or cause a spook, and she couldn't have been reacting to the sidereins, since I had not even clipped them to her bridle yet.

"What's up?" Karla asked as she slid open the big arena door. I must have been shaking my head or otherwise looking bemused.

"She reared," I said. "Flipped over backwards. I can't figure out why."

"DID she?" Karla asked with a gleam in her eye. "Well let's just see what's up then, shall we? Is she alright?"

"Physically, yes," I said. Karla laughed and took the reins.

As Karla sized up the big mare I was reminded of a scene from the movie *Michael*. John Travolta plays Michael the Archangel in the film, come down to earth to help an old lady in her time of need. Now Michael, as the old lady explains, is not your typical angel – ethereal and otherworldly. No, Michael is hairy and a little overweight. He relishes his time on earth in human form for the sheer physicality of it; the eating, drinking, sex and sensuality of it; the taste and smell and feel-against-your-skin of it. All those bodily pleasures not available to him in Heaven. In one scene he fights a bull. Not like a matador, elegantly with a red cape, but rather as if he, too, were a bull. He lines the great beast up in a pasture, rakes the ground with his foot, lowers his head, and with a cry of "Battle!" he charges. The bull launches himself forward in response. They meet with a crash. In the next shot the bull is on the ground and Michael, dazed and happy, is walking from the field.

Sahara stood no better chance against Karla than that bull had against Michael the Archangel.

"The secret is to keep her moving," Karla explained as Sahara did that stunning, floaty trot of hers that made your breath catch in your throat. "She can't rear UP if she's going FORWARD." And Karla applied her legs of steel to make sure Sahara did just that. Go FORWARD. Not UP.

To me the comment seemed to beg the question of what would happen when they had to stop. They couldn't keep moving FORWARD indefinitely, after all. But it seemed wrong to question this cosmic law. In dressage, which was Karla's specialty, you move FORWARD (as well as STRAIGHT). And yes, both words are capitalized even when spoken, and always spoken with a trace of German accent. It's serious business. You also move OFF the leg (yours) and THROUGH the back (the horse's). You have RHYTHM, too, and IMPULSION. And it all sounds fairly logical and easy but in fact takes years to even understand it, never mind actually accomplish it on horseback. Ride your horse forward, asking for a lively, rhythmic, relaxed straight movement with your leg, letting her bring her spine upward, her hind legs under her, her head and neck beautifully arched in front of you and light in your hand. Easy. Right up until you try it and she hangs the full weight of her head and neck on the reins, dragging you forward so you cannot use your seat and your legs properly and she's ignoring them anyway, swinging her butt out to the wall and leaning hard on her inside shoulder like a crabwalking pretzel, laughing at you silently behind those big dark eyes while your coach yells at you to ride FORWARD and STRAIGHT and in RHYTHM. Mere mortals cannot do it.

But Karla could. Under her, Sahara moved like a dream: neck arched, jaw relaxed, shoulders and hips loose and swinging, eyes soft. Foolishly, I hoped to some day get her to do the same for me.

Of course her colic surgery a few weeks later derailed those plans for quite a while. Having hoovered down her afternoon meal of hay, she promptly threw herself to the floor of her stall and began to thrash around. The vet and I were both summoned promptly. It's the phone call no horse owner wants. Colic could be a mild stomach upset caused by a few bites of rich spring grass or an emotional upset, or it could be deadly. The pain often caused horses to roll on the ground, trying to ease their discomfort, sometimes leading to a disastrously twisted gut. Colic could result in an impaction, requiring surgery. Or, as in Sahara's case, it could cause gas serious enough to shift the intestines around, causing a loop to get stranded over the nephrosplenic ligament and trapped against the abdominal wall.

The vet arrived at Willowbrook shortly after I did. He examined the mare and asked a question that was even more devastating than the phone call had been:

"How would you feel about a trip to Guelph?"

Guelph is Guelph University. More specifically, it's the large-animal clinic at the Ontario Veterinary College located at the University of Guelph. One of the finest, and most frightening, equine clinics anywhere. "Going to Guelph" usually meant a horse was in so much trouble they would be the only ones to have even a decent shot at saving her. Often, it was the kind of trouble horses simply did not make it through. It also meant a sizeable vet bill and a two-hour trailer ride. I nodded my head, and away we went.

A quick assessment at Guelph confirmed what the barn vet had suspected. The intestine was entrapped, nothing could move past the point of entrapment, and surgery was Sahara's only hope.

She sailed through the surgery and recovered well. She came out of general anaesthetic without the drama that some horses present, kicking and scrambling, and damaging not only the surgical incision but often limbs and other body parts as well (in fact, some clinics suspend the horse in water while it regains consciousness to minimize the damage). Sahara also managed to avoid the adhesions, infections, laminitis and other complications that sometimes follow equine surgery. All she had to show for her emergency repair was a long incision in her abdomen and a shaved neck with an IV needle stuck into it, the tube braided neatly into her mane. After six months of carefully monitored recuperation, first at Willowbrook and then at my little barn, she would be ready to go again.

We resumed work slowly. Mostly we puttered around the paddocks, doing a lot of walking to build her muscles back up. Sahara behaved respectably, with only an occasional half-hearted hop of her front end in protest of something unpleasant (like being asked to go around the paddock one more time) or scary (like someone closing a car door nearby).

The day she reared again, we'd nearly finished one of our pleasant little jaunts around the paddocks. Christopher had been jogging around on Oscar while I did conditioning exercises with Sahara, walking her up and down little hills and asking her to bend, flex, and generally bring her muscles back into play. I was still working with her when Christopher decided he'd had enough riding and took Oscar to the barn. Left alone, Sahara panicked (or had a temper-tantrum, depending on your perspective), and reared. She had been relaxed and calm and I hadn't seen it coming. I also don't remember it.

I must have smacked my head quite hard when I hit the ground because I don't remember anything between the time that Christopher disappeared with Oscar and the time Robert and I were leaving the emergency room at the local hospital some seven hours later. Despite the helmet, the crack on the head had been hard enough to give me a concussion. Robert had decided to have me checked out after I'd asked him, for the ninth or tenth time: "What happened?"

That's when I sent Sahara back to Karla.

I stick in the saddle pretty well. It takes some effort to dump me, and not many horses have. But Sahara was now playing dirty. "Mare" had become a four-letter word. Besides, I had by now become more interested in therapeutic riding than I was in breeding, and Sahara would NEVER be a therapy horse. I'd have Karla polish her up and sell her. Or maybe Karla would decide to buy the mare herself? She'd never had a horse with Sahara's potential: the extravagant way of moving, the power to do the most demanding work. The mare was spectacular, athletic and showy. You could not ignore her when she strutted her stuff.

Alas, Sahara's limitations turned out not to be physical ones.

"She's dumb as a brick," Karla finally concluded after weeks of riding the mare daily. "As long as I work her every day she's fine, but give her a Sunday off, and on Monday I have to re-write the entire book. Everything's gone. Poof. Vanished."

Dressage is mentally demanding, and no amount of training can make a horse *smarter.* It was time for Sahara to move on. I sold her as a show-hunter. Her dam, after all, had been winning everything on the show circuit for years now, and her grandfather had made it to the Olympics, so jumping was in her blood. It was evident as soon as we put a forward seat saddle on her and pointed her at a jump. Sahara was a horse transformed. Her ears pricked up, her face relaxed, and her stride had an extra bounce in it. Her jumping technique would need work, but she was clearly in her element.

With Sahara gone, I could focus more on Wilby, as well as working with the youngsters. Olivia and Henk were old enough now to start wearing tack and working lightly in the round pen, while the "slaughter house three" needed lots of daily handling to learn their ground manners. I was still making the weekly drive to volunteer with the therapeutic riding program, too, and had pretty much decided that was what I wanted to do with my horses. But that would require an indoor arena. It made no sense to build one in our current cramped quarters, and besides, Robert's itch to own a bigger piece of land kept surfacing every time we took a drive in the country. Every country property with a "For Sale" sign on it drew him like a moth to flame. We started looking for a farm.

We looked at farm after farm, discovering villages and townships we had never heard of. We looked at places that were already set up for horses, and others that would need work to make them equine friendly. We were trying to be flexible, but nothing seemed right. Too expensive. Too big. Too small. Bad location. Swampy. On a busy road. Too far from work. Too close to the local gravel pit… It was an exercise in frustration.

And then we found it. It was March and the place was covered knee-deep in snow. It was in the snow belt of Oro-Medonte, a ten-minute drive from the local ski resort. We could only slog our way into the first of the hay fields, and the real estate agent was a bit vague on the boundary lines. "It's sort of square. Over to that treeline. Or maybe the one past the creek? I'll check and let you know." The house was old and tiny. The barns were decrepit, their ceilings too low for horses. The fencing was no good and would have to be replaced.

We made an offer the same day.

Even covered in snow, the land was absolutely stunning: rolling hills with a stream along one boundary, fields edged by stands of mature maples, and a view of the valley and hills surrounding the farm that took my breath away. Whereas our current property was quickly being squeezed by development with what amounted to a secondary highway in front of it, the new place averaged three cars per hour (I counted) and "a neighbour" was anyone living within five miles. Coyotes yipped and howled in the evening (causing our overly-civilized dogs to tuck their tails and head for the house) and deer and wild turkeys ventured from the bush into the hayfields at dusk. We had found home.

But "home" needed months of work before any of us – four-legged or two – could move in. Buying the property was only the beginning.

I'd read something once about the wine business, which applies equally well to horses: "If you want to make a small fortune in this business, start with a big one." And while we were far from having a fortune to spend, the money faucet had been opened. We soon discovered that with horse farms, as with wineries, the money flows only one way – out.

We hired a contractor to gut and update the house, replace the ancient plumbing and wiring, and to build an addition to accommodate us all. The old house didn't even have heating upstairs – just vents in the floors to allow warm air from the main floor up into the bedrooms. We had geothermal heating installed, the septic system replaced, and built a living room big enough to house a pool table and a big TV. The boys each got a large bedroom, and their own bathroom in the addition. The plan was to finish the basement for more living space, but for the first few years after we moved in it would be used only for storage, and a place for the dogs to hang out. We gutted the upstairs of the old house, turning four tiny rooms into one large bedroom/office and bath, and tore up the linoleum in the kitchen to find lovely, unfinished hardwood underneath. We converted what had been the living and dining rooms into a private sitting room and bedroom for my mother, and had a bathroom built for her. The insulation needed to be upgraded and the siding replaced, the ugly concrete stoop replaced with a porch, the little sunroom insulated and turned into a small but serviceable dining area.

But while I took an interest in the renovations on the house, my real interest was in the new barn we had begun planning. In truth I didn't care how big our kitchen was, or whether the master bedroom had an en-suite. I don't consider myself any sort of "master" at any rate, and have no problem walking down a hall to use the bathroom. And the kitchen? How much room do you need for the dishwasher and the microwave? But how many stalls to build and what size; whether to store hay above them (convenient, but dusty and runs the risk of fire) or in a separate shed (safer but more work); whether to build a conventional steel and wood arena or one of the new steel and cloth buildings – these were challenging decisions!

Naturally, in the end we built too many stalls – thirteen – but wisely did not finish them all right away. We settled on a fabric arena for its wonderful brightness – we rarely turn on the lights in the summer, and only in the evenings the rest of the year. We trucked in tons of limestone screenings as a foundation for the arena footing, and I spent an entire day pushing a compacting machine around to pound the gravel down until my teeth rattled and my hands "hummed" strangely even after I turned the machine off. Many truckloads of sand were spread on top of the base, and eventually treated with an environmentally-friendly dust-control product that also cost a small fortune.

We did as much of the work ourselves as we could, but Robert and I both worked full-time and still had our little farm to run back at the old house. So most of the work had to be trusted to contractors. Our biggest mistake was telling them that they had until the following spring to finish, as we had decided not to move during the school-year, and the end result was that the work stretched on… and on… and on.

So as moving day drew closer, it became evident that the barn would not be finished. The outside structure was done, the posts for the stall partitions were in, but that was about all. There was no wall to separate barn from arena; the hayloft floor was incomplete; the concrete aisles had not been poured; the grading of the stall floors was unfinished; there was no electricity or water. And while the paddocks had been built, the horses could not simply be turned out while their living quarters were completed. Unaccustomed as they were to rich pasture, they would have gorged themselves on their pristine pastures and colicked. What was I going to do with six horses who could not be turned out, and no barn to put them in?

I started making phone calls, hoping against hope to find someone who could take in my herd. I was not optimistic. Most stables have, at most, a stall or two available at any given time. But six? I started with my friend Diana. She had recently moved to a new farm, and I had my fingers crossed, hoping she had not yet filled her barn with boarders. She had. My heart sank.

"But I'll call Christina," she offered kindly. " She might have room. I'll call you back."

I didn't hold out much hope. I didn't know Christina, and had no reason to think she could help. She had no idea who I was, so why would she put herself out? What did she care about some crazy woman who was looking for stabling for SIX HORSES on short notice? But I had underestimated Christina, and Diana, too.

"She can take them," Diana reported back within the hour. "Here's her number. She's waiting for your call."

It turned out that Christina ran a breeding facility. She stood two very handsome, very large Irish Draft horses at stud, and had extra stabling to accommodate the mares that were sent to her for breeding. Since breeding season was over, she had plenty of room, and would be happy to help.

"One other problem," I said, now feeling like I was being a complete pain. "My horses can't go out on grass."

To my astonishment, Christina laughed. "Don't worry," she said, "we're pretty much grass-free around here. You can have your choice of dust-bowls for turn-out."

I stared at the phone in disbelief for a while after I hung up. Had this conversation really happened? Was I saved? Did I in fact have a place to keep the horses while we made their barn habitable?

"You'll never believe this," I told Robert. "I've found a place to keep the horses. We won't have to move them into the house after all."

"What's it going to cost?" he asked.

"I have absolutely no idea." I realized I had completely forgotten to ask.

8

Thought before action, if you have time.
(Dick Francis)

Few things cause more trouble between horses and their humans than trailering. Talk to any horseperson, and they'll have traile-ring stories to tell: about spending six hours trying to convince a stubborn / terrified / cranky / obstinate (fill in your choice of adjective) horse onto a trailer for a twenty-minute ride. They'll tell you about horses arriving in a foaming sweat, quivering with fear and stress, screaming for their friends and flying off the trailer backwards, human handler flapping in the breeze at the end of a leadshank. If you're VERY unlucky, they'll tell you about horrific accidents or minor inconveniences like having a flat tire which turned into a nightmare when terrified horses had to be unloaded on the side of a busy highway while repairs were made.

Of all the unnatural things we make our horses do (like living in 12 x 12-foot box-stalls, carrying us on their backs, tolerating predators like dogs and humans who would send them fleeing for their lives in the wild), trailering might just be the worst. Look at it from the horse's point of view: here is a creature whose very survival depends on being able to run away from danger, being asked to submissively walk into a tiny, dark, foreign metal container with no visible means of escape, a rickety ramp and nasty metallic echoes and then stand there patiently while the tin can bumps and sways and rattles, until someone tells him to get off again – backwards – in a strange place. Now remember that horses are masters of reading body-language and mood, and add into the mix a stressed-out human being who may hate the whole trailering experience almost as much as the horse does, and don't be surprised if that horse expects to die in the process.

One of the biggest problems with trailering is that most horses don't do it very often, and when they do have to get on a trailer, they really HAVE to get on the trailer. They're either moving to another farm, going to a show, the vet, or some other "appointment" that will not wait. That puts extra pressure on the humans involved, since they're under a deadline. There's no time to play around, especially if you're paying for the trailer, truck and driver by the hour!

So long before we had to make the big move, I began introducing the youngsters to the trailer. My idea was to take the "scary" out of the trailer – get them to see it as just another stall, even if this one happened to be on wheels. If I could get them used to the look, the smell, the sound – and get them to associate nice things (like food) with it, then they wouldn't worry when they actually had to go somewhere.

With that in mind, we parked our two-horse trailer in the paddock where Henk and Olivia lived with the herd, and just let them get used to having it in their lives. Henk, of course, was the first one over to examine the red monster even before Robert had unhitched the truck. After sniffing it thoroughly all over, Henk proceeded to look for anything loose (electrical cords, safety chains) that he could chew, rip or otherwise mangle. He bumped the side of the trailer with his nose, pretending he'd scared himself with the metallic "bang" it made, and made sure he left some teeth-marks in the paint.

The adults came over, had a look, and wandered off with bored expressions on their faces. Nothing new here, kids, and no food to be had either.

Olivia, on the other hand, steered clear, refusing to go anywhere near "the thing" and confining herself to the opposite corner of the paddock for days. This did not bode well. However, after a few days, and seeing that the others were by no means afraid of this strange contraption, she sucked up the courage to go investigate. When the trailer didn't bite her, she decided it would be OK to munch the hay I'd left nearby. I decided the time was ripe to go the next step.

I put the grown-ups in the other paddock to keep them from interfering, and, armed with two buckets containing Henk and Olivia's lunches, I dropped the trailer ramp and set up shop. Instead of catching the horses and leading them to the trailer, I simply let them come to me. Once they arrived, I let them have a bite of grain, then backed up a bit so they had to step onto the ramp. Necks stretched out long, lips smacking, the two babies tried out the ramp with their front feet. I let them finish their lunch.

Next day we repeated the exercise, but this time they had to come farther up the ramp to have their lunch. No problem. They followed the grain and happily mowed down once I let them have the buckets.

On day three, I decided to lure them all the way into the trailer. We followed the usual routine, but after a couple of bites of food, I moved the buckets back into the trailer. Again they followed. I smiled. This was easier than I'd expected!

That, of course, was my critical mistake. Even before the thought was fully formed in my mind, Olivia swung her butt to the right for no apparent reason, her hind leg slid off the side of the ramp, and she was gone, whirling away in a flash of brown and white and galloping off to the far side of the paddock. Startled, Henk pulled his head out of the bucket and looked after her. For a moment it looked like he would take off after her, which is what most horses would do. Not Henk. He happily stuck his head back in the bucket and followed me as I backed farther into the trailer. Who needed Olivia? He was probably calculating how much more grain her departure might get him. I took another step, then another, and Henk was all the way inside now, still happily munching away. I told him what a good boy he was, and let him finish his lunch.

When the last of his grain was gone, I put the bucket down and clipped a leadshank to Henk's halter. I didn't want him to suddenly realize where he was, now that the distraction of the food was gone, and fly out of the trailer backwards. Instead, he stuck his nose in the crook of my arm and stood still, happy to just hang out with his human for a while, enjoying himself as I scratched behind his ears and in front of his withers. He let out a long sigh and stamped a hind foot to get rid of a fly, contented as he could be.

"OK, Henkie," I said, giving a little push in the middle of his chest, "let's see if you can walk off this thing."

Step by step, as relaxed as can be, he backed down the ramp and into the paddock, checking only briefly to see where Olivia was. She stood in the same spot she'd run to earlier, watching intently to see if the red monster had eaten her buddy for good and evidently relieved to see him come out alive. Henk whinnied and she walked over tentatively, touching noses with him to make sure he really was OK. He butted her with his head, then turned back to me and gave me a push with his nose.

"Oh, you want more, do you?" I asked laughing. "OK, let's see you do it without the food."

I backed into the trailer slowly, and he followed. No fuss, no nerves, no bribery required. To say I was impressed would be an understatement of the highest order. I made a big fuss over him, gave him a handful of grain out of Olivia's bucket, and backed him off again. Amazed, I unclipped the lead shank and turned him loose. He didn't go anywhere. He stood by, occasionally trying to butt in as I fed Olivia the rest of her grain while she stood tentatively with both front feet on the trailer ramp, her body tight as a wound spring, ready to leap away and run to safety at the first sign of the red monster trying to gobble her up.

The next day I locked the big guys up in their own paddock again and opened up the trailer. Henk cantered over immediately while Olivia kept her distance. Putting the feed buckets inside the trailer this time, I clipped the lead to Henk's halter and asked him to walk onto the trailer with me. He did. I backed him off, loaded him again, gave him lots of pats and let him eat his lunch standing in the trailer. Then I backed him off and turned him loose. He had done everything asked of him and was free to go and relax. Olivia's turn.

I put on her lead shank and led her to the trailer. She followed quite happily, looking trusting and relaxed, and walked her front feet up onto the ramp. Then she stopped and dug in her heels. Instead of fighting her I stopped, let her eat some grain and think about things. She relaxed visibly and took another step. I was ecstatic. More eating, more stroking and quiet, encouraging words, then another step and halt. Her head was now inside the trailer, her front feet at the top of the ramp, but she refused to step up with her hinds, instead stretching her body and neck to reach me while keeping those back hooves planted on solid ground. She simply stopped. She didn't fight me, but did not co-operate, either. It was the proverbial line in the sand and she refused to cross it. I decided not to force her, still intent on making the experience a good one. I let her finish her lunch, gave her lots of pats, and turned her loose.

By now the horses had figured out the routine, so by the time I'd separated the big guys and opened up the trailer the next day, both youngsters were eagerly looking for their lunch. I put the food inside, led Henk on and off the trailer a couple of times and fed him. He was happy, grunting as he ate, his eyes half-closed with pleasure. Olivia looked impatient, poking her head inside the trailer looking for her food, but in no way inclined to come inside and get it. She carefully skirted the ramp, standing off to the side and craning her long neck to poke her head into the trailer. When I unloaded Henk and brought her to the ramp, she had to go through her whole little routine all over again, testing out the ramp first with one delicate little hoof, then the other, and stretching as far as her lanky body could go to reach her bucket without committing those back feet to the ramp.

I sighed, trying very hard not to lose my patience. I knew that teaching a horse something new could take time, but I wanted to see at least a little progress. Slowly, without any pressure, I coaxed her forward, talking reassuringly and offering treats (admittedly, by this time I was calling her some fairly unflattering names, but they were all uttered in a gentle, caressing tone that made them *sound* sweet and friendly, anyway). As I focused on the filly, I could see Henk hanging around, watching the proceedings, his ears pricked forward and a look of intense curiosity on his face, as if he were trying to figure out what was bothering the big filly. Then he, too, seemed to tire of her game, and coming around to his side of the trailer he walked up the ramp and stood inside, nosing around on the floor for any fallen bits of food. He snorted some dust out of his nostrils, satisfied himself that all the food was gone, and backed off down the ramp again as if someone were directing him with an invisible hand. He stopped at the bottom of the ramp and gave Olivia a bored look as if trying to impress upon her just how easy this all was.

I could hardly believe what had just happened, and burst out laughing at the look on his face. Big mistake. The filly spooked and flew backwards off the ramp, yanking on the lead shank, trying to get away. I managed to hold her but only by bracing hard at the bottom of the ramp. I was still laughing, though. Henk stood by, watching. He reminded me of one of those students we all seemed to have had in class with us at one point or another – the kid who not only got the math questions first, but pretty quickly figured out a whole different way to find the answer – the kid that make the math teacher scratch his head in wonder – the kid who looked with a degree of pity at the rest of us, unable to understand why we found the work so mysteriously difficult.

Olivia and I went back to square one, because now I had insulted her by laughing and Henk had showed her up in a most unflattering way. I inched my way back up the ramp, keeping things friendly and relaxed and grateful for every little bit of "give" from the filly, watching her body language to make sure she wasn't beginning to stress out. Meanwhile, Henk loaded himself into, and unloaded himself out of, the trailer several more times. It was a game now, apparently. He was actually enjoying himself. Thankfully, some of his happy mood rubbed off on Olivia, to the point that she eventually walked into the trailer and ate her food. I was so happy I would have given her a hug, except I knew that it would send her flying off and we'd have to start all over again. She was in the trailer, but she was not entirely thrilled about it, and I noticed that her back feet stayed on the ramp, ready for a quick getaway at the first sign of trouble.

Close enough, I thought. It was that progress I had been looking for. Within a few days she would walk all the way in with hardly any hesitation, and look relatively relaxed doing so. We hauled the trailer back out of the paddock before Henk could finish removing its paint, and only did a few refreshers from time to time so the kids would not forget that the trailer was their friend.

I repeated the exercise with Moose, Ronan and Rosie, and was thrilled to find the "slaughter-house three" were almost as easy with their lessons as Henk had been. Not surprisingly, Ronan expressed the greatest concern about the trailer, eyeing is suspiciously at first and "breathing fire" through distended nostrils. But he got over his fear quickly, largely due to Rosie's non-chalant attitude about it all. The big grey filly was positively happy about the process. "Food? Just for standing around in this box? Cool!" Having discovered the wonder of grain, apples, carrots and the like, Rosie had become very food motivated. Scotch mints were her absolute favourite, so these were reserved for times of maximum stress – the vet, the farrier, learning to wear a saddle for the first time. Rosie, and to a lesser degree Moose and Ronan, too, would do almost anything for a mint.

Winter turned out to be particularly nasty that year. Freezing rain turned the paddocks into skating rinks for weeks. I'd muck the stalls each morning and spread the soiled shavings and manure on the ice to give the horses traction, but hold my breath each time I heard a hoof skidding along looking for grip. Weeks of snow-storms followed, filling the sand ring and round pen with too much snow for the plough to deal with, so all training came to a halt. I called Willowbrook to see if they might have a stall for Wilby, and it turned out they had three. One of their clients had taken his horses to Florida for the winter, and I was welcome to "sublet" his stalls for a few weeks. I decided to take Henk and Olivia along with Wilby. It would do the youngsters good to get off the farm and see some new sights.

Naturally, "shipping day" was disgusting. The radio called them snow squalls. I called it a blizzard. Wind whipped the snow around, driving it up my sleeves and down my collar, and into my eyes and nose. Pulling a trailer in this weather would be an unprecedented joy. We considered postponing, but the next day was expected to be worse, and Robert had taken the day off work to do the driving. We waited until after lunch just in case the weather improved in the afternoon and, amazingly, it did just that. The winds calmed and the snow stopped almost completely.

We loaded up the truck with feed, extra halters, blankets, and everything else the beasts might need, walked Wilby onto the trailer, and pulled out of the driveway. Henk and Olivia trotted along the fenceline, following the trailer as far as they could, then watched with their heads hanging over the fence while we drove away. I wondered what they made of the whole thing. They had watched Sahara disappear the same way when I'd sent her back to Willowbrook to train with Karla, and of course she never came back. Did they think Wilby was about to disappear forever the same way? But Oscar was unconcerned, eating hay, and the "slaughter house three" did not seem too worried, either.

We settled Wilby in his stall and drove home to find the two youngsters still waiting by the fence. Olivia's face, when she whinnied and got no response from inside the trailer, clearly said: "See? I TOLD you that thing would eat him!" She gave Henk a reproachful look. He merely looked bored.

When I put the lead shank on Henk and led him to the trailer, he walked right on and stood there, waiting for the filly. She, of course, decided to start her trailer training all over again, one tiny step at a time. After a half hour and no more than half of

Olivia on the trailer, we took Henk back to the barn to keep him from freezing. An hour later, I called the girls at Willowbrook to bring out the heavy artillery – a tranquilizer. If we could just take the edge off the filly's fears, we reasoned, she might decide to walk on as she had done in the summer.

Wrong.

First with Henk, and then without him (you can only ask a horse to hang around on a cold trailer for so long), we coaxed and pushed and prodded and bribed and threatened the now slightly stoned filly – to no avail. There were four of us now, Karla and Jamie kindly offering to stay and help. Between them, they had loaded more temperamental show and race horses than either of them could remember. They knew every trick, and tried them all: the nonchalant walk up the ramp, the chain over the nose to discourage backing up, the lunge line behind the rump, two lunge lines to create a corridor up the ramp, the lunging whip, the broom, the nice talk, the tough talk, the careful lifting and placing of each individual hoof on the ramp, the carrots, the grain, the natural horsemanship tricks and games and…. nothing. Olivia was drugged and fairly mellow, but now entirely, mulishly, stubbornly refusing to even consider putting those lovely back feet of hers on the ramp.

It was getting dark, and we were beginning to consider calling it a day when the filly decided the matter for us. Whether the drugs had worn off or she simply decided she'd had enough she reared high – very, very high – lost her balance and flipped onto her back, smacking her head on the ground. For a moment she lay still while everyone's heart stopped. Then she scrambled to her feet as we rushed towards her to find a sizeable wound on the side of her head where she had hit a hard chunk of snow. She looked shaky as she walked back to the barn, and we would need to monitor her for a few hours to make sure the injury was no worse than split skin. Much to everyone's relief she settled happily in her stall, sticking her nose through the bars to say hello to Henk.

Next day we tried again. The weather forecast was turning ugly later in the day with no relief in sight. We had to get the youngsters to the farm today. Robert booked the morning off work, and we started nice and early. Karla and Jamie came to help, and, since Olivia had recovered nicely from her fall, we started with her, leaving Henkie in the barn. Since the tranquilizer had accomplished little the previous day, we decided not to try it again. Instead we removed the centre partition, giving her the entire trailer as a target instead of one skinny side of it, and tried again. The familiar routine: walk up to the ramp nicely, then balk, lean entire weight back until almost sitting on the ground, then decide it's OK to stand up straight and put one foot on the ramp, then the other, then lean all the way back again and give a meaningful roll of the eyes, straighten up and seem to relax slightly, moving the first foot further up the ramp and after much begging, prompting and cajoling from the humans shift the other foot up to join it. Then, when it looks like this might finally be the time when those hind feet will follow and the entire horse might go up and in, fly out backwards, dragging whoever is holding the other end of the shank out too, and stand snorting and upset in the snow, blowing steam and quivering dramatically. We were getting nowhere and my frustration level was reaching a critical point. This mare was simply not going to walk onto that trailer.

Then Jamie had a brainstorm. If Olivia refused to go forward, maybe she would back onto the ramp? At the moment reverse seemed to be her preferred gear, and while it sounded unorthodox, Jamie had seen it work before, and it was certainly worth a try.

We turned Liv around at the base of the ramp and quietly asked her to back up, which she happily did. I expected her to panic as her hind feet touched the ramp but she didn't. Instead, she lifted up one foot and then the other, placing them halfway up the ramp's incline – something we had not managed at all until now. Then she took another step and another, and then her front feet were on the ramp too, and still she seemed content. Thrilled but still waiting for her to clue in to what was going on and fly off at any moment, Jamie kept asking for the backward steps while the rest of us guided Liv's rear end into the trailer. Without the centre partition there was plenty of room, and without stopping or even a hesitation, Olivia walked on. Backwards. Then she stood still.

We closed the back of the trailer in record time, still waiting for the realization: "AAAARRGH! The trailer!" and the mad rush to get off. Nothing. She stood, more relaxed than she'd been since breakfast. We looked at each other in stunned silence. She was on the trailer!!!!

Now there was only the small matter of turning her around. We briefly considered leaving her as she was. There are actually studies showing that horses prefer being shipped backward and, given the chance if left untied, will turn to face the back of the trailer by themselves. But there was no safe way to tie her at the back end, the trailer being a standard two-horse designed to carry horses facing forward, so we decided to turn her around. In the end it proved relatively easy. Although big, Liv was only two and relatively compact compared to what she would be as an adult, and with a little scrambling she managed the one-eighty quite handily. Still calm. It was as if, once she'd lost the battle, she'd given up entirely and decided to be very mature about the rest of the proceedings.

Still we were not prepared to test her new-found serenity by opening the trailer to load Henkie, so off we went to Willowbrook, leaving the little black horse to wait his turn. He whinnied when we came back into the barn to get him finally, clearly relieved that we had not abandoned him forever. Never one to hold a grudge, he walked onto the trailer sweetly, taking his revenge only by opening the escape door at the front of the trailer three times on the short trip from our farm to Willowbrook. He had never done that before and has never done it since. I swear he knew we'd taken shameless advantage of his sweet nature, and he was just letting us know it.

When I came out to Willowbrook to ride Wilby the next day, I naturally asked how the horses had settled in – as expected, nicely – and whether they had behaved themselves. Much to my surprise, this caused Karla to giggle in a most uncharacteristic way. She controlled the laughter, but still looked sheepish.

"What?" I asked when it looked like she wasn't going to answer. "What happened?"

Now Karla burst out laughing and laughed until she cried. She couldn't answer then, even if she wanted to. She laughed until she had to lean against a wall. She tried to get herself under control and then started to laugh again, helpless to contain herself. She laughed so hard that a couple of boarders who'd been cleaning their saddles in the tack room poked their heads around the corner of the door to see what was going on, and Jamie walked out of the stall she had been mucking to check the situation out. When she saw Karla and me, her eyebrows shot together in a frown.

"Oh, very nice," she said. "I see Karla's been telling you about my little adventure with your horse."

Karla wailed and slid down the wall to sit on a tack trunk, helpless with laughter. Jamie scowled some more while I looked from the one to the other like a fool, trying to understand what was going on.

"What adventure?" I finally asked. "Which horse? I don't know anything. She can't talk!"

"Henk," Jamie said with a distinct edge to her voice. "He nearly dragged me into the next county this morning."

"What?" I was incredulous and mortified. I hate it when horses are disrespectful, walking all over their humans. It's certainly not something I tolerate in my animals, and didn't like to hear that Henk had done it to Jamie.

"Yeah, seems I made the mistake of leaving him till last for turn-out. He'd been so good. Mellow, even, so I didn't think anything of it and took everybody else outside first. Then I put his lead shank on, opened the door, and away we went!" Jamie explained, and I was relieved to see a little twinkle of amusement in her eyes. She was not completely angry.

"She was just kind of hanging on…" Karla sputtered. "Like a waterskier behind a boat. He nearly lost her in the doorway. And then he dragged her through this huge snowbank!" And then we lost her again as the vision of Henkie and Jamie plowing through three feet of snow turned out to be too much to bear and she dissolved into a fresh bout of laughter.

"Oh, my god, Jamie, I'm so sorry," I said, glaring at Henk as he stood in his stall, all innocent perky ears and deep soulful eyes. "He's not usually like that at all."

"Well now I know better," Jamie said. "After she stopped laughing at me, this one," she indicated the giggling Karla with a toss of the head, "informed me that that's why you rarely see women working on a Friesian farm. 'Cause if one decides he's going somewhere, it's pretty hard to persuade him to change his mind. They weren't bred to pull stuff for nothing. They just throw their heads in the air and go."

"I think it's like shutting your eyes when something scares you," Karla said, wiping the tears from her face. "You just close them and go. Hope for the best. He was more scared than he looked, I think, and just wanted to be with the others."

"Well you'd better believe I'm going to be ready for him tomorrow," Jamie said. "It's a good thing he's been sucking up to me all afternoon to make up for it."

And that was when I found out that even the perfect Friesian could have an occasional imperfect moment.

9

*There is something about the outside of a
horse that is good for the inside of a man.
(Winston Churchill)*

Fortunately for me and for the riders in my therapeutic riding program, those imperfect Friesian moments are pretty rare. By the time he was five years old, Henk had joined Oscar and Wilby in the therapeutic riding program.

Five is pretty young for a horse. A five-year-old horse can be scatter-brained and skittish. Not having much experience in life, a young horse often finds things frightening that an older horse would not. I couldn't imagine Oscar as a five-year-old, for example, being any good for a beginner of any sort, never mind one with extra challenges to deal with. No, Oscar had only become a suitable therapy horse once he passed his twentieth birthday and decided that spooking and being silly was probably more trouble than it was worth.

But Henk had been a joy to work with from the start. He accepted all parts of his training as he had the trailering lessons. Once he understood what was wanted, he was happy to comply.

Trot around the round pen? No problem. Wear a saddle? Bridle? Sure, why not? You want me to leave my friends and go with you into the big sand ring? OK. The worst he did was untie my boot laces while I was picking out his feet. Henk is obsessed with human footwear. His reaction the first time I finally put my leg over his back and sat in the saddle? He turned his head all the way around, swaying a little to balance the unaccustomed weight, had a look at me sitting up there, then sucked the toe of my boot. Considering the many options he had available to him, I was pretty happy with that one.

My program grew quickly as word got out that therapeutic riding was once again available in the area. The only program that had existed locally had been closed down years before, and nothing had come along to replace it until Robert and I opened the barn door at Stonegate Farm. I hooked up with another instructor for our first year of operation – one who had worked with that other program years ago, and who had some quiet, reliable horses we could use in addition to Oscar and Wilby – and we ran the first few sessions together. It worked well enough, but I soon found the lessons becoming too busy and hectic. With two instructors, as many as five horses and riders and up to fifteen volunteers in the arena at one time, the noise and activity levels could be overwhelming, especially for those riders with Autism whose tolerance of distractions was pretty low to begin with. I wanted a slower, more relaxed pace in my program, and more personal attention for every rider. The program I had originally envisioned had been on a much more intimate scale – more like a yoga session than an aerobics class, but we had strayed from that vision as people had come knocking on the barn door

The move from volunteer to instructor (as well as horse trainer, groom, stall mucker, floor sweeper and… oh yes! college professor trying to earn enough money to keep the whole thing going) had been a big one. Now I had to make the tough decisions. In fact, all the decisions. Who would ride which horse, which exercises were best suited to each group of riders, how many times to ask for a halt or circle before "practice" became "drudgery" during a lesson. It was challenging, but I enjoyed the excitement and newness of it all. I structured my sessions in eight-week blocks as Elaine had done, with children riding one hour per week. Lessons ran in the evening, as dictated not only by my teaching schedule but the work and school commitments of my volunteers. Some riders could come to only a single session, while others would continue to ride for years. Eventually we would add other programs, like the five-week intensive sessions with their little mini-horseshows, and even a summer camp. But that first year I stuck closely to the basics, and gladly paid my "associate instructor" to add some "been-there-done-that" experience, even if it meant my lessons would not be quite my own, or quite the way I wanted them to be.

I stuck it out for that first season, but the following year I started working on my own. That meant I would need another horse to use. Was Henk ready? I had a volunteer ride him in lessons to see how he would react. Was he mentally ready for the work? He answered that question pretty quickly. He loved it. His volunteer rider did everything she could think of to upset him, flopping back and forth in the saddle, sitting off balance, flapping her arms around, and still Henk was relaxed and happy. She played "catch" with one of the other volunteers – occasionally letting the ball hit Henk "accidentally," she threw stuffed animals into buckets, rings onto cones, and joined in the games of "What time is it, Mr. Wolf?" along with the other riders in the group. Henk took it all in stride. This horse was a natural. By early summer he was a regular part of the program and to this day he enjoys the work more than any of the other horses. While Oscar has become a "steady Eddy" and Wilby gallantly complies with whatever is asked of him, Henk enjoys his therapeutic riding lessons even more than he likes going for a trail ride. For a horse that loves people, having the undivided attention of a volunteer leading him, plus one or two others helping the human on his back, and then all those people fussing over him, brushing his gleaming coat and feeding him treats afterward, life just does not get any better.

Henk's very first special-needs rider posed an interesting problem. Tamara very much wanted to ride, but that first step – actually getting on the horse – was daunting. With Tamara, we were hoping for several different outcomes from riding, both physical and psychological. She had a number of developmental issues that sometimes made human relationships (among other things) quite difficult, but she related well to animals. Riding would provide exercise and recreation, and also improve her ability to focus and work toward goals. We hoped that a good relationship with a horse would also translate into better communication with the volunteers and the other riders in the program, leading to a long-term goal of better social skills in general. Riding had much to offer this young woman – if only we could get her on the horse! Putting her leg over the horse's back and then settling into the saddle intimidated her. Like a diver standing at the edge of a sea-side cliff who can't quite take that final step off the preci-pice, Tamara would stand on that mounting block, lift her leg and almost put it over, and then back off. Time and time again.

Her first night with us, it took Tamara twenty minutes to work up the courage to sit on her horse. Twenty minutes standing still at the mounting block is a very long time for any horse, and we did give Henk a few walking breaks, letting him stretch his legs and look around a little. But most of that twenty minutes that wonderful five-year-old stood beside the mounting block, flirt-ing with the volunteer in charge of leading him (nuzzling her hands, lipping her jacket and hair, tucking his head into the circle of her arms for a hug), giving his young rider time to decide that, yes, it was safe after all to swing that leg over his back and let him carry her around the arena.

When she finally sat in that saddle and got underway, Tamara relaxed a little. But only a little. I sidewalked with her for the first few circuits of the arena and she kept a death-grip on my arm, tensing up each time Henk lifted his head, turned a corner or snorted. And each time she tensed, she dug her heels into that horse's sides with a vigour that – had it been me riding – would have sent Henk into a brisk canter around the arena. But with Tamara, he just kept walking, ears relaxed and swiveling back-ward and forward, alternately focused on his leader in front and the sidewalkers behind, one foot hitting the ground after the other and the other and so on in a steady, unbroken rhythm.

And Tamara has kept on riding. She let go of her sidewalkers' arms eventually, and then the saddle, too. She learned to trot down the long side of the arena, pick up the reins and steer Henk through a series of pylons, and halt on command. She does her warm-up calisthenics (mounted, of course) and keeps her heels down, back straight, eyes focused between Henk's ears as we work. Her attitude has gone from a surly bossiness to pleasant co-operation. She is well on her way to exceeding all the goals her parents and I had set out for her before that first lesson. After she dismounts, Tamara helps her volunteers groom Henk and put him in his stall for the night, then feeds every horse in the barn from the bag of sliced apples she brings with her.

Like many of our riders, Tamara came to Stonegate through a community service organization which supports special-needs children in our area. The recreational program is coordinated by a wonderful, over-worked, stressed-out woman named Maggie. Sometimes, riding is a last hope activity for children whom Maggie has placed in other sports and camps without much success. Harry is one such young man.

Diagnosed with Autism, Harry does not communicate with words, and it can be difficult to know just how much he understands of what others say to him. He has trouble focusing on tasks, and prefers not to interact with others. The last camp Maggie had enrolled him in proved a disaster. Harry simply lay down on the floor and refused to participate in anything.

Harry's Mom brought him out to ride without any great expectations. Some Autistic riders refuse to even enter a barn or put on a riding helmet on their first visit, and we had expected Harry to be one of those. Only through small steps – a little more each week – did we think we would actually get Harry to come and ride a horse. To everyone's surprise, though, Harry quite happily put on his helmet, mounted Oscar, and spent the entire hour riding – his very first week here! And while he did lots of looking around at the birds flying near the roof of the arena and the occasional cat meandering along the top of the wall, he was co-operative and seemed happy. Each week, Harry paid a little more attention to his riding and tried more of the exercises the group was doing – stretching forward and back to improve his seat and balance, steering the horse with the reins. By the end of the session he was even staying a while after his lesson to give Oscar a carrot and a few strokes with a brush – major progress for this particular rider who, like so many children with Autism, has sensory issues that make them over-sensitive to touch and smell.

The next time Harry went to camp, he participated in everything. Maggie attributes the change in attitude to his experience with riding.

Connor is another rider I am particularly proud of. He came to us as part of one of Maggie's groups, for a short 4-week session designed to give the kids an opportunity to try out different sports to see what they might like to participate in. Maggie warned me not to expect too much from Connor. He had tried many different sports, but never stuck with anything. Having to wear a brace on his left leg, and with a left hand that did not always co-operate as it should due to Cerebral Palsy, Connor found it difficult to keep up with other kids in the sports he had already tried; a difficult thing for a twelve year old boy to deal with. He would usually start a new activity, attend once or twice, then drop out of the program.

When Connor missed his first lesson with us, I began to suspect we might never see him at all, but he surprised me by showing up in week two. The first horse he saw when he opened the barn door was Wilby. He headed straight for the big gelding's stall.

"Can I ride that horse?" he asked me, pointing to Wilby.

Stroke of luck. Wilby was the horse I had intended to put him on. Wilby is a majestic horse, and riding him is an experience you don't soon forget. All that power under you, that big, arched neck in front, the way he moves – my guess is that Connor had never experienced anything quite like this before. Suddenly, instead of having only two legs – one of which did not work as well as he would have liked – he had four immensely strong ones carrying him anywhere he wanted to go. Instead of a boy who could not keep up with the other kids, he was a boy on a horse that could do things most of the other kids at school could not. Connor is still riding with us. He can ride Wilby with a leader, and Oscar independently at walk and trot, even riding a few basic Para-Equestrian dressage tests of the sort he would perform should he ever decide to take part in competitions that can eventually lead to the Paralympics. These days, Connor does most of the grooming and tacking up himself despite that uncooperative left hand.

Jonathan's mother found me through a complicated web of acquaintances, but I almost turned her down in spite of all that effort. Her son was only four when she first phoned me, and we usually don't take riders under six. Younger than that, and children generally do not learn much from riding. Besides, our horses are quite large, and short legs have a hard time fitting around them. But Heather was persuasive. Jonathan was doing physical therapy now where his workers kept encouraging him to pretend he was "riding a horse" – when sitting on a big exercise ball, for example, working on his sense of balance and strengthening his core muscles – so why not try the real thing, she said. I had to admit it made some sense.

Since Jonathan's challenges were primarily physical – underdeveloped muscles and core strength, poor sense of balance and motor skills – I decided to put him on a horse and see what would happen. Age would not be as much of an issue in his case, since he could benefit from the horse's movement just by sitting there. He didn't have to learn to ride yet. Learning to ride wasn't the point. So I invited Heather to bring Jonathan to watch one of our regular lessons and see if he showed an interest riding. We could then put him on a horse for a few minutes if he wanted to try it, and assess whether or not regular riding might make sense for him.

Jonathan was tiny for his age, and absolutely adorable. He never took his eyes off the horses while he watched the other children ride, and when his Mom asked him if he'd like a turn, he marched right up to the mounting block as he had seen the other riders do. No question. This boy was keen!

We used a thick pad and vaulting surcingle with handles instead of a saddle, and I decided to put him on Henk. The lack of a saddle made Henk somewhat narrower, gave Jonathan two large handles to hold onto, and would challenge his balance and muscles more. Wearing a helmet and sitting on a sixteen-hand horse, Jonathan looked like a little pea on top of a pumpkin. But he was all smiles. Henk seemed to walk extra-carefully (though

I was surprised he even knew there was a rider on him), and my volunteers and I were smitten. Jonathan rocked back and forth as Henk moved underneath him, but he held hard to the handles on the surcingle and kept his balance even through the pylon course.

"OK," I said to Heather. "If he'd like to come back and you'd like to bring him, we'll put him in for four lessons. Then you can decide if it's worth continuing."

Jonathan gave Henk some apples he'd picked from his tree at home, and said he'd like to come again the next week. He was soon learning how to use the reins and doing all the calisthenics that the "big kids" did. By the end of each lesson he would be exhausted. The horse's movement as he walks is huge for a child his size. One week, he fell asleep while riding!

Heather signed Jonathan up for session after session although the drive from her house to our farm was over an hour each way. She bought him a helmet and a few small brushes for Christmas his second year of riding. Jonathan would brush Henk after every ride, standing on a stool so he could reach higher than the top of Henk's front leg. He would hug that leg, too, to say goodbye at the end of the night, and Henk would stand perfectly still until Jonathan was done.

Jonathan's Mom changed jobs recently and had to move. Now the drive is two hours each way and much too long to manage on school nights. And besides, one of the best therapeutic riding programs in the province is ten minutes from their new house. I told Heather to switch, much as I knew we would all miss Jonathan. When they came to say good-bye to Henk, we gave Jonathan a final ride and then let him brush his buddy. He hugged Henk's leg and told him he was the best horse in the world, and I have to agree. When you watch an eleven-hundred-pound horse turn his head and change direction at the request of a thirty-pound boy pulling on his rein, you just have to smile and give that horse an extra carrot with his dinner.

10

*We are each of us angels with only
one wing, and we can only fly
by embracing one another.
(Luciano de Crescenzo)*

The satisfaction that comes from putting smiles on the faces of children who have little enough to smile about, is obvious. It's one of the things that makes even getting up at 5:30 to feed and turn out the horses before heading off to work, or finishing up those last late-night chores after an evening of lessons, worth doing.

For me, the *un*expected benefit of therapeutic riding is the people I get to meet.

Talk to anyone involved with therapeutic riding, and they will tell you that the most difficult part is finding volunteers. And it's true. It takes up to three volunteers per rider to do a lesson safely – one to lead the horse, and one or two to sidewalk, offering physical support as needed, but much more, too. Because some riders process information more slowly than others, the sidewalkers may need to re-enforce what the instructor has asked riders to do, or correct a mistake. They encourage the rider to try harder, and to take a chance on trying something new. They provide a comfort-level by being there, close-up and paying attention, and the consistency so many riders crave by working with the same child every week, week after week.

And it's not easy work, either. Hot in summer, cold in winter, our volunteers spend two one-hour lessons back-to-back walking and running beside the horses in sandy footing that's great for horses' legs and feet but less well suited to two-legged humans. And it goes without saying that some riders pose more of a challenge than others: those who try to leap off the horse's back without warning, those who like to pull hair, take off their helmets or lie down on their horse, those who get angry or stubborn or who simply shut down part-way through a lesson and need to be coaxed / cajoled / drawn out of their shells diplomatically to re-engage with the group and the work at hand. Volunteers need athleticism, stamina, resourcefulness and patience!

While there are nights when we're so short-handed that I pull parents in to help, and teach the lesson while also sidewalking with a rider, most of the time we are lucky.

Several of my "regulars" have been with the program since it started, working virtually every session and even putting themselves "on-call" for nights when they're not scheduled to work but are ready and willing to pitch in if someone calls in sick. They put the word out, too, to friends and riding buddies (many of our volunteers are riders), or bring their teen-aged children along to help. Some drive long distances to get here, and willingly re-arrange their schedules to suit ours. They come with treats for the horses, hand-me-down riding clothes for the riders, and used tack and equipment for the program.

This love of horses, and a desire to help others, are about all our volunteers have in common. They range in age from thirteen to fifty-eight. Some are high-school students who take riding lessons at the local lesson barns, others are in college studying to be veterinary technicians, recreational therapy practitioners, social workers, personal support workers or police officers. Many of the college students have horses "back home" whom they miss terribly. Some volunteers are horse owners, recreational or competitive, while others are recently retired and finally in a position to indulge a passion from their youth. Some, like Krystal, start out as riders in our program and then begin to volunteer. None of them complain about the heat, the cold, or the unpleasant sensation of having sand in their shoes (Dooley is particularly skilled at flicking his front feet "just so" to deposit the maximum amount of sand down the back of your shoe or boot). They'll pull double duty when someone is away, and happily find extra chores to do like sweeping the barn or hanging water buckets in the stalls on the occasional night when too many volunteers show up or a rider is away.

For those who don't have their own horses, volunteering in our program gives them a chance to spend time in a barn; an odd desire by some people's standards, but one any horse lover can understand. A volunteer who lives down the road and whose family had horses while she was growing up summed it up perfectly one night when she walked through the barn door, took a deep breath, and declared: "I wish I could bottle up this smell and take it home with me." We all laughed and nodded. We knew exactly what she meant.

Early on, while I was advertising in the local paper for volunteers, a woman I had never met arrived with a trunk-full of blankets, saddle-pads, a bridle or two, and *apologized* for having nothing more to give me. She lived too far away to make the drive to volunteer, she said, but had rounded up what she could find from friends at her barn to give me for my horses.

Another supporter of the program invited me to visit friends of hers (who turned out to be one of Canada's most prominent international riders and his wife) at their gorgeous new farm. There we rummaged through a tack-room full of gear accumulated over decades in the horse business, free to take whatever we thought might suit.

"Use what you can, and sell the rest," they told me. "We know what it costs to keep a horse."

What it costs to keep a horse, indeed. Horse keeping has never been cheap, and with fuel and feed prices climbing, it's becoming more expensive all the time.

People who don't own horses look at what I'm doing and get excited:

"What a great way to earn a living! Helping kids. Working with horses. When are you going to quit your job and do it full-time?" they'll ask me.

"When I win the lottery," I tell them. "Therapeutic riding is NOT a money making proposition. The lessons barely pay for the horse feed, never mind the mortgage, the insurance, the electric bill, the vet, the food for the humans in the household…"

And it's the high cost of keeping horses that leads to the other form of donation people like to offer to our program – the horse.

I've been offered all manner of horses, usually by well-intentioned people, most of the horses unsuitable, and many with stories that can break your heart. The old mare who's standing in a pasture doing nothing because her owner died and his widow cannot afford to keep her. The former show horse who has injured himself or simply grown too old for the show-ring. The unsuccessful racehorse that may not escape the slaughter house if we cannot take him in.

I find myself explaining to people that it takes a very special horse to do therapeutic work. Just because a horse has finished his show career or grown too old to jump does not mean he will take happily to therapeutic riding lessons. Old or sore does not necessarily mean patient and forgiving. And that three-year-old that's proven to be too slow for the race-track or too small for the show-ring would take years of training to prepare for therapeutic work, *if* he has the right temperament in the first place. So usually I say "no." There is a limit to the number of mouths I can feed.

But two of our best therapy horses are, indeed, donations

Dooley is an ancient Appaloosa whose owner had bought a younger horse for showing, and could not bear to see the old boy standing around with nothing to do and no one to give him the attention he'd been used to. I trust Dooley with my most vulnerable riders, knowing he will take the best possible care of them. Out in the paddock when he's not working, Dooley faithfully follows a boarder's mare around, smitten with unrequited love.

Harley was donated to me by a woman who could no longer keep him. A retired Standardbred racehorse, Harley shows all the signs of a long career at the track: legs covered in surgical scars and the tell-tale white hairs that result from pin-firing. While sound enough for therapeutic work and the occasional trail ride, Harley would likely break down under heavy riding. For me, the bonus is that his long racing career exposed him to sights and sounds most horses never experience, and he is both unflappable and sweet-natured. Our only problem with Harley is that he trots so fast, that I need very fit volunteers to work with him in any lesson that will involve anything faster than a walk!

Star A third "donation" ended up with one of my volunteers. I simply could not take another horse, but this old mare's story was distressing – she likely faced euthanasia if a home could not be found. So I told Valerie about her. A few comments Valerie had made had led me to think that she was ready for a horse of her own again after many years without, and this gentle mare could make a lovely trail horse for her. Valerie said "yes." Star now gets her coat brushed twice a day, special supplements are added to her feed to help her gain lost pounds, and her pictures are proudly shown off at every opportunity. She has made a very soft landing!

Those who want to ride get a chance to do so, either by warming up the horses before a lesson, or coming out on days when the lesson horses are not working to give them a little schooling and light exercise. The recently-purchased Canadian horse Louis, in particular, needs exercise between lessons, and several volunteers are happy to oblige. Being a Canadian (the national horse of our country that too few people seem to be aware of), Louis is bold and brave and full of personality. But he puts on weight more easily than most, and also needs to be reminded from time to time that he is a horse and not in fact a human. Regular work under saddle with a skillful volunteer rider helps to accomplish both.

As a therapy horse, Louis proved his value almost immediately. A group home had contacted me about an adult client they had, who had done some riding before and expressed a desire to ride again. Could we accommodate him? I scheduled him into a lesson and selected Louis for him to ride. All went well while we got the horses ready and mounted the other riders, but the moment Louis' rider was up and the horse took a few steps forward, his rider had a melt-down. He flailed his arms and legs and yelled, trying to jump off the horse while managing to tangle himself in his stirrups and reins. The volunteers sidewalking with him did a masterful job keeping him from falling, while I untangled him from the tack (a job made more difficult by the fact the young man did not tolerate being touched). Finally I was able to dismount him from Louis and take him back to the workers who had brought him, all of whom professed surprise at his reaction. Through it all, Louis had stood quietly, swiveling his ears towards the commotion on his back but otherwise unflinching. Needless to say, his grateful leader and sidewalkers gave Louis many extra carrots as a "thank you" that day.

Because they are living creatures and not bicycles or gym equipment, the horses demand special skills from the volunteers. They need to learn each horse's unique quirks. Oscar, for example, nips when his girth is tightened, and likes to flip his head up and down when the rider's reins or the leaders lead shank pulls too hard on his mouth. Henk, having figured out that the centre of the arena is where we halt to play games, discuss new exercises or horsemanship questions ("show me your horse's mane…"), and dismount at the end of a lesson, will usually halt there on his own, even when the current plan is simply to cross the arena on a diagonal and change direction. Dooley, left to his own devices, will cut corners and wander towards the centre of the arena, and he rarely trots the entire length of the long-side unless actively encouraged to do so. Harley needs to be convinced to line up correctly at the mounting block, and must be led into his stall at a very specific angle. Having smacked his hip on the stall door once he does not wish to repeat the experience. He also became quite nervous the first time he worked an evening lesson in the fall. We finally figured out that he was frightened of the shadows he cast on the arena floor once the lights were turned on – shadows that seemed to follow him around and flitted around his feet.

Being prey animals whose first defense is to run away, even the most unflappable of horses can be frightened from time to time. Volunteers must be prepared, and ensure the safety of their riders. Perhaps the scariest experience I've had in working with disabled riders took place before my own program was up and running, while I was volunteering with another instructor. I was sidewalking with a young rider whose challenges were so severe that he required the sidewalker to hold him in place on the horse. The lesson was progressing smoothly when a light-bulb directly overhead in the arena suddenly exploded. The horse spooked violently, and it was all I could do to lift the rider off the horse safely before she flew away sideways. You couldn't really blame the horse for reacting, but it must be said that she calmed down long before the instructor, leader, or I did!

As I've said, our volunteers need to be truly special, and they are. I am sincerely thankful for their generous spirit and willing hands. I enjoy their company and draw strength from their enthusiasm. I know – and try to make sure I tell them that I know – that the program would not be possible without them.

11

*Riding a horse is not a gentle hobby, to be
picked up and laid down like a game of
Solitaire. It is a grand passion.*
(Ralph Waldo Emerson)

Just like the unsuitable horses I am offered by strangers looking
to "re-home" a horse they can no longer use, I realized before
setting up the program that some of the horses we already had
in our own herd would not work out as therapy horses, either.
Once the decision had been made to find a farm and establish
a therapeutic riding program, we had to think about what we
would need in the way of horses to do the job.

Sahara, the ultimate anti-therapy horse, had already been sold
to a young woman with dreams of ribbons and trophies from
jumping competitions. Good thing, too, for here was a horse in
need of some therapy of her own – NOT a candidate for therapeutic riding! That was one problem taken care of. But as she
grew older, it became evident that Olivia would not fit into our
new plans, either. Breeding sport horses was no longer in our future, and, like Sahara, Olivia was a prima dona. A diva. A drama

queen. The world – whatever world she was to live in – would need to revolve around her. She made that plain with her trailer-loading antics, and if there was any doubt at all left in our minds, she eliminated it by developing ulcers shortly after her little "vacation" at Willowbrook.

When she became ill, the vet and I of course suspected colic. Olivia was lying down, looking tense, and in obvious distress. Over the next few days the vet would treat her for colic, watch the filly improve enough to leave for his next appointment, only to be called back again after the filly's very next meal, with our lovely young mare presenting precisely the same symptoms all over again. She would lie on her side groaning, feebly waving a foreleg in the air, the very picture of misery that would indicate in almost any other horse a digestive upset of the magnitude that had sent Sahara to Guelph for surgery. But Olivia was not colicking and had certainly not twisted an intestine. By process of elimination the vet finally treated her for ulcers.

The diagnosis took a while, because Olivia was by no means an obvious candidate for developing ulcers. As in people, ulcers in horses are usually caused by stress, and aggravated by diet. Ulcers are most often found in race horses and competition mounts; horses whose lives are defined by stalls and trailers, rigorous training, the stress of competition, and a feeding program designed to maximize energy. These horses rarely enjoy a day in a paddock with friends and their feed consists of buckets-full of grains and supplements. Olivia developed ulcers while doing nothing more stressful than going outside in the morning to munch grass or hay, coming in at night, being groomed, and having the farrier trim her feet every six weeks or so.

The pharmacist gave me a strange look over the top of his reading-glasses when I presented the prescription to him.

"Who is Olivia Tepera?" he asked, frowning at the very large dosage in the prescription, imagining, I guessed, a mountain of a woman…

"My horse," I said, and noticed the relief on his face. "Evidently horses and humans use the same meds for ulcers."

The good news was that a few weeks of medication cleared the ulcers up, and that Olivia liked her meds. After I mixed them with maple syrup and shot the sweet mixture into her mouth with a needle-less syringe, she smacked her lips and looked for more. Soon she was tackling me each time I entered her stall, looking for more of her special treats.

"OK," I said to the vet as we watched the now-recovered filly beating up Henk in a corner of the paddock, "what am I doing to make her life so stressful?"

"Nothing," he said. "Some horses are just more tightly wound than others. They'll work themselves up into a sweat because someone's moved their water bucket to a different place in their stall."

I laughed.

"I've seen Olivia do that," I said.

"It's evident from the way she reacted to the pain," the vet went on. "I've treated racehorses that have lived with ulcers for years and you'd never know it, except that they'll sometimes go off their feed and get skinny. No thrashing on the ground and rolling their eyes and begging for drugs. Some are just more stoic. Others need to be the centre of attention. It's pretty obvious which one your mare is."

Keeping Olivia as a pleasure horse would be like using a Ferrari to deliver pizza – overkill in the performance department along with an impractically high maintenance bill. Besides, I was beginning to suspect my life was about to become rather hectic ('though I still underestimated just HOW hectic it would be), and there would be no place for a demanding diva in that schedule. I offered her to Jack, who owned both Willowbrook Farm and Kelly, the mare I had leased and bred to produce Olivia. He had fallen in love with Olivia during her stay at Willowbrook the previous winter, and thought she could make a wonderful jumper. He bought her happily, but she eventually turned out to be too much trouble for him, too. Last I heard, Olivia was living the quiet life of a broodmare in Maryland, producing lovely show-horses. This would be a lifestyle she would enjoy – pampered mom. I was happy she had found her niche in life.

That left "the boys" and Rosie. Oscar and the two Friesians would all work in the program (once Henk was old enough). North went back to Willowbrook where Karla was still working. Of the "slaughter-house three," I thought that Rosie had the most potential as a therapy horse once she was older and fully trained, with Moose a possibility, though his immense size would limit his usefulness. Ronan was unlikely to ever settle enough to be a truly reliable lesson horse of any sort. But selling any of these three was not an option I was prepared to consider. They had come perilously close to the slaughter house once already, and I was not going to take the chance that it could happen again. So whether they ever came to earn their keep or not, these three horses were coming with us.

All three "PMU babies" had begun working in the round-pen and wearing tack before we moved from our old farm. Once we moved to Stonegate I gave them a refresher course on the lunge-line occasionally, and planned to start getting on and training them from the saddle once they turned three years old. More demanding training would start only once they were four and more or less fully grown (though Moose would continue to grow until he was six!).

Moose co-operated fairly well with my plans, though doing *anything* with this massive horse proved to be a pretty good workout. I'd ridden lots of big horses before, but Moose takes BIG to another level. He stands 17 hands high at the withers, and it's a huge 17 hands. He weighs 400 or 500 pounds more than your typical 17-hand Thoroughbred or warm-blood, and it all seems to be muscle. One flick of his head while you're putting on his bridle can send you skidding across the barn floor. He likes to lean all his weight on you while you are cleaning out his feet, and if he lifts his head to look at something as you're leading him, he can pick you right up off your feet. Plus he's a coward. A lilly-livered chicken despite his size. "Yellow on the outside (he's a lovely palomino colour), yellow on the inside," as my friend Jill would say. And this means constant vigilance on the handler's part, since a Moose spook can have you dragging across the arena on the end of the lunge-line in a heart-beat if you're not ready for it. He is a difficult horse to stop.

I would find out just *how* difficult one day in early spring. I had been riding Moose fairly regularly for about two months by then, and felt relatively comfortable riding him on my own. Not that I had much choice. An extra pair of hands is extremely helpful while training youngsters, but I'm usually on my own. Despite the advice I read once in a book on starting young horses that suggested the earliest training should be left to "the groom," and that various jobs should be delegated to one's assistant, I ended up doing pretty much everything myself. Grooms? Assistants? The author of that book is clearly not living in *my* world!

My lack of regular help in starting the youngsters proved to be a particular pain with Moose, who liked to fidget and fuss and walk off while being mounted. Sometimes, with no one to hold and steady him, I would spend a frustratingly long time just persuading that massive beast to stand still while I got on.

On this particular day, Moose stood relatively well to be mounted, but my rear end had barely touched the saddle before he took off at a run. I managed to jam my feet into the stirrups and started trying to brake, but no luck. He was off! As he picked up speed, I remember the thought flashed through my mind that his canter was remarkably comfortable for a horse of his size and breeding. But soon it wasn't a canter any longer, and an out-of-control gallop inside an arena on a seventeen-hand horse is anything but comfortable! He was banking in the turns and picking up speed with every stride. Pulling on the reins had no discernible effect. I tried all the emergency-stop techniques I knew: pulley-rein, riding in a small circle, turning the horse into the wall. Nothing. I braced in the stirrups and pulled with all my strength on one rein, but he barely seemed to feel it. It occurred to me that a loose-ring snaffle (the mildest of bits) was perhaps not enough for this big horse. I decided on the spot to put him into something more effective if I survived the ride. As we threaded the needle between the mounting block and the wall (Moose's decision, not mine), the vision of a spectacular crash played briefly in my mind. I wondered if we'd leave one of those perfect outlines of ourselves as we went barreling through the wall, the way Wylie Coyote always did when chasing the Road Runner.

Deciding not to find out, I took a deep breath, focused all my energy, and pulled on that right rein with everything I had. Finally I saw the big roman-nosed head turn. We circled, slowed, then stopped. I took a deep breath and told Moose he was a good boy for stopping, but as I reached forward to stroke his neck he leaped forward and off we went again! It took less work to stop this time. I suspect Moose was getting tired, and a good thing, too, because I was nearly out of steam. We walked around the arena a couple of times, did some very basic schooling, and I jumped off. My arms were weak and my legs like jelly. Partly it was from the sheer effort of stopping that horse, but partly it was the experience of being out of control. Never, in all my years of riding, have I been physically unable to stop a horse at will. It's an experience I hope never to repeat, and to help make sure of that, I've upgraded Moose's snaffle to a bit with a curb chain. Just in case.

I racked my brains for days to understand what had happened to set Moose off. As far as I could recall, there had been nothing unusual or startling to spook him: no dog jumping on the Dutch door between the barn and the arena, no gust of wind or "whoosh" of snow sliding off the roof. I ran through the whole sequence of events over and over in my mind, trying to pinpoint a cause, but could find none. Nothing. Just swinging my leg over, touching butt to saddle, then "Go!"

And then it came to me. As so often happens, like when you're trying to remember someone's name or the title of a song, and you've almost given up, and then it comes to you while you're doing something completely different, I suddenly realized while mucking stalls a few days later, what had been different that day. My jacket. The weather had begun to turn warmer, and I had put on a different coat. A poor choice, apparently, as the lighter coat had an outer shell of nylon that made a funny sound when I moved, not like the polar fleece coat I'd been wearing through the winter. When he heard that noise behind his head, Moose had lost his cool. The nylon monster was about to eat him. And it was already on his back – the place where mountain lions attack their prey by leaping from above. He was expecting the fatal bite at the back of the neck. Every time he moved, he'd hear the rustling and freak out even more. When I'd hauled him to a stop and reached down to pat him it happened again, and off he went.

The nylon coat "retired" for the time being along with the snaffle bit.

Mystery solved. But it was clear Moose would not be ready for therapeutic work anytime soon. As he matured, I hoped, he might overcome his in-born cowardice and become the kind of steady, dependable mount that many draft-cross horses are, but I didn't expect it to happen quickly. That was fine. Once he learned enough for Robert to be able to ride him, Moose would be his horse. In the meantime, several of my volunteers were enjoying working with the big gelding, teaching him to trot over poles and even jump small obstacles. His walk, trot and canter were all very pleasant to ride – springy and soft, and he tried hard to do what was asked of him as long as nothing was threatening to eat him.

Rosie posed a very different sort of training challenge: she needed to understand which one of us – horse or human – was in charge. Once that small issue was resolved, she became a smart and willing student who progressed quickly in her training.

The sorting out of who would call the shots was fairly dramatic, though. In the early days of serious training, I judged our progress by the number of times Rosie broke the cross-ties. As a safety precaution, I have always attached the two ropes by which we "cross-tie" our horses in the aisle for grooming and tacking up by several loops of binder twine. That way, should a horse panic while tied, the twine will break and hopefully keep the horse from hurting itself (or, in the case of Moose or Rosie, pulling down a wall!).

With Rosie, it wasn't really ever a question of panic, though. She seemed to find excuses (girth being tightened, someone walking through the barn door behind her, a bird singing in the tree outside…) to plunge forward, head high, butt low, cross-ties barely slowing her down as she snapped the twine. She never went far. Once free, she'd turn back towards me, cross-ties dangling from her halter, with a "So there!" expression on her face. I learned to simply climb a stool, re-attach the cross-ties to their rings, re-attach Rosie to the cross-ties, and finish what we'd been doing before her break for freedom. After a time she seemed satisfied with a single episode per session, and eventually she stopped altogether, evidently having grown bored with this particular game.

The more interesting game would take place once we reached the arena for a lesson on the lunge-line. Rosie lunged beautifully. To the left. Walk, trot, canter, halt. She did it all. But to the right? That simply was not going to happen. She would start off for a few strides, maybe even a complete circle or two, and then she was done. She would slam on the brakes, spin around, and trot off in the opposite direction. Side-reins did nothing to stop the spin.

I would reel her in, turn her back in the correct direction, and start again. And she would repeat the performance. When she got particularly mulish about it, turning her back to the right could become a death-defying stunt. She knew that once I got a position beside her right hip I would be able to drive her forward in the direction she so hated, and she would do anything to keep me from getting there. We had numerous stand-offs, with Rosie spinning repeatedly to face me like a fine-tuned cutting-horse, trying to keep me away from her right side. If I persisted she'd run through me or over me if I wasn't careful to prevent it. This was clearly a dominance issue, and I couldn't let her win. I also couldn't get angry. That would accomplish nothing. There were many days when the two of us would square off in that arena like prize-fighters in a ring, trying to guess each other's next move and ready to foil it. On the worst days, just getting to that right hip and driving her around me a few times in the right direction was a victory. She was fourteen hundred pounds of determined, stubborn horse.

In the end, I won.

It took weeks of work and a depth of patience I don't usually possess, but I won. Eventually she gave in as she had with
the cross-ties and simply began to work in both directions. She
would occasionally try a spin just to see if I was paying attention,
but the effort became more symbolic than serious. She gave in
easily when I blocked her. Her expression was almost playful.
"OK," she seemed to be saying, "I'll play along. Just don't let
your guard down!"

Once we established who was running the training program,
Rosie took to the work as though becoming a riding horse had
been HER idea. She lunged, long-lined, stood quietly at the
mounting block, tolerated the feed bags I tied to her saddle and
her stirrups to simulate a rider's weight and to bump against her
sides as she lunged. Her ears were mobile, her expression soft
and relaxed. When I slid my leg over her and settled in the saddle
she shifted to adjust her balance, then stood quietly. She learned
the aids to walk, turn and halt, and we were soon doing a few
circuits of easy trot, as well. While not as springy as Moose and
with none of Ronan's extravagant floatiness, Rosie turned out to
be a comfortable ride, and certainly a pleasant one. Even the occasional spook when snow slid off the arena or the wind rattled
the big outside door was not spectacular, and easy to stop. No
crazy bolting or shoulder-dropping attempts to dump her rider.
Rosie, I thought, would make a lovely therapeutic riding horse
some day.

Not so Ronan. While Moose and Rosie remembered most of their early training, Ronan evidently retained little of his. He stood politely to have the saddle and bridle put on as he had been taught months before at our old farm, but once I tightened the girth even slightly he hunched up his back and leaped straight up into the air. He landed, did it again, then bounced around the barn like a massive four-legged pogo stick. Boing, boing, boing he went, head down, tail tucked, back arched, four feet off the ground. Boing.

When he got it out of his system and let me lead him to the arena he lunged nicely but never relaxed. Cats in the rafters, snow on the roof, dogs in the barn – anything could set him off. But not always. The thing that he found terrifying one day would barely make an impression on the next, then send him bucking again two days after that.

There would be no question of my trying to back this horse myself. While I'd enjoyed such death-defying stunts once upon a time, I no longer "bounced" that well. Having a silly youngster put me out of commission was not something I could afford, and getting dumped wasn't as amusing now as it had been when I was twenty. No, Ronan would be sent to a professional trainer. And when he returned from there with a barely passing grade and a caution to work him everyday or risk a blow-up, he went back into the paddock to be pasture art until there was more time to decide what, if anything, to do with him.

In the meantime, we rounded out the ranks of the working therapy horses with Louis, the little Canadian horse with the big attitude, Dooley the sweet old Appaloosa who was losing his eyesight but not his gentle demeanor, and Harley the retired Standardbred with the big, kind eyes. Between them, these six horses (Oscar, Wilby, Henk, Louis, Dooley and Harley) would look after all our riders, big and small.

There was, briefly, a seventh lesson horse – a small Quarter Horse who'd caught our eye when we were test-riding Louis. Diesel seemed to have a lovely attitude and solid temperament. He'd had little formal training but had been ridden out on trail rides instead, and seemed kind and unflappable enough to be considered for the program. We brought him home along with Louis and put the pair of them into the capable hands of two volunteers from the college. Tammy and Shawna were far from home and their own horses, so they pampered Louis and Diesel shamelessly. They groomed them until they gleamed, braided their manes, polished their hooves and taught them to eat muffins. More importantly, they spent the winter putting miles on the pair of them, giving them the training they would need to handle therapeutic riding. They introduced them to the games they'd be expected to play during lessons, and how to stand very still while their riders worked on their stretching exercises.

Eventually the little horses graduated to working in lessons, but while Louis took to the work like he'd been bred for it, Diesel soon proved himself too unpredictable to work safely with our riders. I was just starting to think about selling him, when Helena mentioned that her parents wanted to buy her a horse. Since "graduating" from her session with us more than a year earlier (all the practicing of the that dressage test in her backyard had paid off and she'd done the whole routine beautifully in our little horse show), Helena had taken some lessons off and on and now volunteered with our program one night a week. She was a very capable rider, and certainly able to manage a horse like Diesel. She tried him out, loved him, and the deal was done. She boards him at our farm, and Diesel is back to having just one special human in his life as he'd had with Tammy.

It's a joy to watch Helena and her little horse together. I think that having an animal to look after brings her great happiness. A horse is nothing like a dog, with its slavish devotion to its master. If a horse deigns you worthy of his trust and affection, it is a very special thing. And I know that when Diesel gives Helena that look – the "you're *my* human and I choose to be with you" look, it makes her feel ten feet tall. I know this, because it happens to me, too. When I drag myself to the barn after a crazy day jammed full with too much to do and too many people all wanting a little piece of me, all it takes is to get that look from one of my horses and I feel restored. It is a healing thing indeed, the deep dark kindness of a horse's eye.

12

*There are only two emotions that
belong in the saddle. One is a sense
of humour, and the other is patience.*
(John Lyons)

Sometimes life's coincidences are so weirdly, perfectly timed, that
they make you wonder if they're coincidences at all. Sometimes,
when the timing is propitious and several things happen together, you notice things you probably should have realized anyway.
Sometimes, you just need a smack over the head to make you
pay attention. And so it was with me.

I had picked up a book called "In Praise of Slow: How a world-
wide movement is challenging the cult of speed." Having spent
a couple of decades working in the hyperdrive environment of
the consumer electronics business, I could relate. The author's
musings on the effects of speed – at work, at home, on the road,
while eating, playing or making love – rang true. I'd been there,
grabbing a bite to eat over the kitchen sink before flying out the
door instead of sitting down to dinner and enjoying some time
with the people I loved; drumming my fingers on the steering

wheel while waiting for a group of school kids to cross the road instead of enjoying the music on the radio and the lovely sunshine pouring in through the car windows. A tight knot of stress always in the pit of my stomach.

The author, Carl Honore, explained that he'd realized just how caught up he'd become in the cult of speed when he'd actually considered buying a book called "The One-Minute Bedtime Story." He'd found this little gem at an airport bookstore, the ultimate haunt of the time-starved: a business traveler rushing from someplace to someplace else and bogged down by a delayed flight or missed connection. The book, Honore said, "condensed classic fairy tales into sixty-second sound bites. Think Hans Christian Anderson meets the executive summary." Thinking how handy this could be for shortening his young son's bedtime ritual, Honore was actually on his way to the cash register, book in hand, when he had a moment's clarity and realized what he was doing. That near-brush with time-deprivation hell had been the genesis of his own book.

I read with interest about Honore's journey through the worlds of Yoga and Chi Kung, two ancient practices that taught the art being in the moment, tuned into the present, and modern movements of Slow Food and Slow Cities, part of the growing revolt against fast food, the MacDonaldization of global cultures, and the emphasis on speed. I found myself nodding in recognition at the workaholics he described and also the epiphanies he'd experienced while learning to hold a Tree Pose. And it dawned on me as I was reading that time-deprivation is a uniquely human thing. Animals don't suffer from it. And much as we try to infect them with this very modern illness, they're simply too smart to play along. I realized, suddenly, that Henk had been trying to teach me this lesson for some time now.

In the summer, the herd was out on pasture in a large field some distance from the barn. This meant a longish, time-consuming walk to get a horse if I wanted to go for a ride. I soon discovered that if my chosen mount for the ride was Henk, the greater my hurry, the slower he would be on the walk back to the barn. I would charge into the paddock to grab him for a quick ride before I had to teach a lesson or hop in the car to pick up my kids from football practice, and Henk would refuse to rush along with me. He would very politely let me clip the lead rope to his halter, but as soon as I started marching off, trying to hurry-up-and-let's-get-to-the-barn-as-fast-as-we-can, he'd plant his fuzzy black feet and stop, let me get to the end of that lead rope and realize I'd left the horse somewhere in my wake. I'd then have to backtrack to where I belonged, back beside his head, and invite him to walk with me. He'd happily do so, his head bobbing beside my right shoulder, right up until I started to rush again and get ahead of him. Then he'd stop, lift his head in defiance, and wait for me to come back to him once more. Some days it made me want to cry with frustration, but I would never get mad at him because he was right. When I slow down, start breathing properly, quell the "gotta-go-gotta-run-run-run" demon in my belly, I enjoy my time with my horse much more. And if there's no enjoyment in it, then what's the point, anyway?

Sometimes the whole herd teaches me a lesson. On a lovely June day this summer I had an appointment for the vet to come and vaccinate the gang at 1:30. My last class at the college ended at 12, giving me lots of time to get home, change into my barn clothes and bring the horses in before Ed arrived. What I hadn't planned on was a stream of students stopping by to ask questions about an assignment, and the photocopier jamming when I needed to run off a quiz for next day's 8 a.m. class. It was 1 o'clock by the time I burned rubber out of the school parking lot for the twenty-minute drive home. The adrenalin was pumping as I turned onto the highway, but I tried to calm myself with the thought that vets were *never* on time. Unless you had the first appointment of the day you were guaranteed at least a half-hour wait. An hour was more likely. Work at other farms always took longer than expected, and if an emergency came up, all bets were off.

Naturally, this day would be the exception that proved the rule. I saw Ed's truck approach from the opposite direction and turn into my driveway just ahead of me. Perfect. I threw on by barn clothes and ran to the far pasture while Ed organized his gear at the barn. I could have left the horses in the barn paddock that morning where they'd be close at hand, but I'd decided to be nice and let them out in the big field where the grazing was better and the trees provided shade from the midday sun. Now I'd have to move them across the laneway from the pasture to the paddock, then catch them as they came to the gate nearest the barn and bring them in.

They must have sensed my stress-level, because they kept their distance. Horses who normally mobbed me when I entered the field now moved away as I jogged toward them. I slowed down and Wilby turned his gentle head toward me, taking a few steps in my direction. I could have kissed him. Where Wilby went, the rest of the herd would follow. Once I moved him to the other paddock, the rest of them would wait by the pasture gate for their turn. He was the herd leader after all.

But not this day. While Wilby galloped across the paddock toward the barn, the rest of the horses stayed put, heads down, grazing, but watching me with wary eyes. They would force me to walk down the hill and catch each one of them, lead him up the hill to the gate, transfer him to the paddock, then walk down the hill again to fetch the next horse. Not one horse came voluntarily to the gate that day. Not one. They took one look at my impatient jog down that hill, saw the tension in my body, and knew I was going to be no fun that day. Was it their fault I was keeping the vet waiting? They were in no hurry to pay the price for my bad planning.

And it's even worse when we rush our horses in their training. Being human, we feel the need for daily progress – a steady movement along some road we've planned out in our minds from "horse who knows nothing" to "horse who reads our minds." We have a plan, a system, a program we want our horse to follow and that's great. Training needs to be organized and structured. We need to build new skills onto old ones the horse already knows. But we can't forget that a horse is a living creature, not a bicycle, and progress won't always go in a nice straight line with predictable improvements every day. A horse can have a bad day, just like a human can. A horse can forget, get confused, become too preoccupied with that pretty mare our friend is riding in the arena with us to focus on getting that shoulder-in just right.

So then we have a decision to make: is it really necessary to perfect that shoulder-in today, or should we just invite our friend to bring her pretty mare outside and go for a nice long trail ride with us? We can stay the course and fight, and likely finish our ride angry and frustrated, or we can let perfection wait another day and just enjoy our horse's company.

Of course there's a fine line between tuning in to your horse and working in synch with his ability to learn, and giving in to obstinance or bad behaviour. But then, no one ever said that training a horse should be easy! Go too far in either direction, and you end up with a mess of trouble on your hands.

Around the same time I'd started reading Honore's book, I received an email from my friend Stella. The email gushed about an attached video that I simply HAD to watch! The most amazing dressage performance! A dressage rider herself, Stella liked nothing better than to watch high-level competitions, and she'd found this video on YouTube, documenting a recent World Cup ride by some up-and-coming star.

I clicked on the link and watched as a truly lovely horse began the demanding movements of his test. He was magnificent. He carried himself like royalty. His extended trot seemed to hover above the ground. He danced through his tempis (a "skipping" movement where the horse changes canter leads at every stride), and flowed through the half-pass, moving like a ballet dancer on a stage. I caught myself smiling.

And then the spell was broken. Asked for Piaffe (a very physically difficult trot in place), the horse became tense and his tail swished from side to side. His ears were no longer mobile, alternately pricking forward with interest and cocking back attentively toward his rider, but now stayed back, not pinned in anger but distinctly unhappy. Instead of a graceful ballet dancer he now resembled a weight-lifter struggling with a weight that's just beyond his ability to lift. His movements were jerky, his expression tense. The unhappiness continued through the Passage (a very collected, almost slow-motion trot) and the canter pirouettes. To me, the exercises looked forced and stilted, more like cheap circus tricks than the highest expression of equine grace and equestrian art. And always that swishing, wringing tail, that tense unhappy face. I felt let down.

I closed the attachment and hit "delete" without responding to Stella's email. From what I could see, the horse was not ready for the Grand Prix movements he was being asked for, and his obvious unhappiness made it hard for me to watch. Telling Stella the truth would start an argument, but I couldn't bring myself to lie. I hoped Stella would forget about the email, but no such luck. Inevitably, she brought it up the next time saw each other.

"Well, what did you think?" she demanded. "Wasn't that incredible?" She was evidently annoyed at my lack of response to her e-mail.

I tried to be diplomatic, I really did.

"That's one stunning horse," I said.

"But the ride. Wow. Wasn't that about as good as it gets?" She would not leave it alone.

"I don't think I'd say that, no."

Stella speared me with a look.

"What do you mean? Why not?"

"It looked… I don't know… Forced. The horse doesn't look happy." I was trying to keep the depth of distaste for what I'd seen out of my voice, but knew I was in dangerous waters now.

"What do you mean, 'not happy'?" Stella demanded.

"His tail's swishing. He looks really tense. He looks like he'd rather be doing something else. Anything else."

"All dressage horses' tails swish," Stella said.

"Well, that's my point, really." Like the fool I am, I plunged into the deep end. "I wondered if that was true and I was just over-reacting, so I hit YouTube. I thought I'd have a look at the Lipizzaners at the Spanish Riding School. 'Cause to me, dressage just doesn't get any better than that. And you know what? In all the performances they've got posted up there, from working in-hand with the young stallions right up to the Airs Above the Ground, there's not a single angry tail-swish or a pinned-back ear or a horse that looks like he'd rather be somewhere else. They all look… happy. And then you go to videos from the big dressage shows and half the horses look like they hate their jobs."

"Maybe Lipizzaners just have a different attitude," Stella countered.

"Or maybe it's because they've been trained more slowly and given the chance to develop and mature." OK, I was asking for it now. Stella was starting to look as cranky as the horse in that video, but I plowed on. "Did you know," I challenged my angry friend, "that they don't even bring the stallions in from the stud farm until they're four, and don't do the advanced stuff with school stallions until they're ten? There was a tribute on the website to a stallion they'd just retired from performing. He was twenty-seven! Have you EVER seen a dressage horse in this country who could do that?"

Stella wasn't buying it, but that was fine. I wasn't really out to convert her. But I was pretty sure I was onto something, because as I thought back to when Stella and I had both started riding as kids, it had been a given that horses didn't start any real training under saddle until they were four. Before that they were babies, and only learned about ground manners: leading, tying, having their feet done – maybe a little work on the lunge line wearing tack, but not with a rider on their backs. You'd usually get on them in the fall of their three-year-old year, then give them the winter off, and start work under saddle the following spring.

Now we were starting two-year olds, and some were even competing under saddle at that age. People were just not willing to keep a horse that wasn't working that extra year or two. They had to "earn their keep," ready or not. When I was a kid, that had only happened to racehorses.

These poor souls, everyone knew, started their training as babies. By the time they were two, they were pounding their way down racetracks and often retired to the breeding shed before the age of four. Lucky them, if that was their fate. The unlucky ones would keep pounding those tracks until they could run no more.

If they were too damaged to make useful riding horses, they would often end up being sent to slaughter. Rare was the trainer or owner who could afford to retire a used-up racehorse.

And that was the final coincidence. A young woman showed up in my driveway with a borrowed truck and trailer, her five-year-old thoroughbred gelding in the back. She was desperate for a place to board him for a while, as the farm where she'd had him for the past few months was becoming unsafe, she said, with fences falling apart and bad hay that was making her horse sick. She'd been sent my way by a friend of a friend who happened to know my husband. I told her the horse could stay until she found another place to take him, and I'd reduce her board to a price she could afford if she'd help with chores a few days a week. She was obviously relieved, and we took the little gelding to the barn.

The injury was immediately obvious. The horse had only retired from racing the year before, following surgery to remove a bone chip from his knee. The knee was twice the size it should have been, but he seemed to be walking fine. It was only when I saw the young woman riding the next day that I saw how lame he really was.

"I think he needs more time off to recover," I told her. "That leg's still very sore."

But she was not prepared to listen. She planned to train the horse, she said, and sell him. For that she had to ride, and so she rode. And rode. She even took the horse out to the back field for a gallop. I cringed at the thought of the pounding that poor knee was taking, but he was not my horse. I could not force her to stop riding. Finally, I suggested it was time for her to leave. I wasn't prepared to be part of that ugly scene.

Now she looked upset. She'd advertised the horse for sale, she said, but there had been no interest. She hadn't found another place to board him, either. Not one she could afford. Would I be interested, she asked, in buying him for the therapeutic riding program? At this point she plunked herself down cross-legged under the gelding's belly to show how quiet and trustworthy he was. And he was all that, I knew. I'd been handling him for weeks and he was one of the sweetest, sanest horses I had met. A pussycat. But I didn't need another horse at the moment. And what about that leg?

I decided to pay for x-rays and some good advice from my vet. I had no great expectations, but if there was a chance the leg could heal enough for light work, maybe we could offer him another chance at a decent life?

Ed looked skeptical as soon as he saw that knee, but he took a full set of x-rays anyway. I wasn't surprised when he called a few days later with bad news. Bone chips were floating in the joint, and arthritis was already well advanced. Not what you want to hear about a five-year-old. As usual, Ed refused to give a definitive answer. Yes, it was possible that after sufficient time off to heal he might be sound enough to work with my smallest riders. On the other hand, there was a very real possibility that he would never really recover and ANY work would be too much. Chances were good that he would end up a very young, very expensive pasture ornament with on-going medical bills.

"It's a classic racing injury," Ed explained. "A joint breaking down because it was asked to do too much too soon. Before it was even fully formed. Sometimes surgery can save a knee like this, but it has to be given time to heal. This poor horse just never got the time he needed."

I turned him down. I was not in a position to take on his expenses. Two days later the young woman was back with the same borrowed truck and trailer and the little gelding left my life as abruptly as he'd entered it. I hope against hope that he found a decent life somewhere, but I doubt it. The odds were stacked against him from the start.

By now I was starting to see the forest that the trees had kept from me before, and it had to do with taking the time that things needed. *Tempo giusto,* as Honore would say. That didn't mean always being slower: sometimes it meant moving on, as when my fast-thinking playful Henk, or an autistic rider for that matter, began to tire of an exercise and needed something new to stimulate him. It also meant allowing yourself to enjoy the process as much as the end result. To have a sense of humour and not see every obstacle as a major catastrophe.

That's probably more important in riding than any other sport, because as a rider, you will NEVER know everything. Every ride can bring a fresh surprise when you're working with a living, breathing, thinking, feeling creature rather than a machine. There is always some new challenge to deal with or new puzzle to figure out. While riding a bike or motorcycle or snowboard is about the laws of physics and A plus B equals C, riding a horse has a healthy dose of unpredictability thrown into the mix and

A plus B *might* equal C today, or it might be the opposite of that for a change, or it might be something altogether unrelated. You'll find out when you try.

This makes riding a mental challenge as well as a physical one. If you give your horse the correct aids for a particular manoeuver (say trotting a nice, round, 20-meter circle) and he responds with something else (the possibilities are limited only by your horse's creativity, but can range from bucking to performing a half-pass or a lovely collected canter), your job is to decode his behaviour and figure out just *why* he responded as he did when both of you know that he understands a 20-meter circle perfectly well, thank you very much, and knows the aids that go along with it. And of course you also need to analyze your own performance to figure out if perhaps you did not ask correctly this time. Did you use too much outside leg? Was your weight shifted too much to the inside? If we're honest with ourselves, we will admit that most horse "mistakes" are caused by the horses' riders.

The same rules apply to figuring out how to entice your horse to walk (gallop, leap), past that boulder beside the trail that he passed without turning a hair yesterday, or why that blue oxer you've been jumping for weeks must suddenly be avoided at all cost. Just because he's done it before does not mean he will do it again!

One of the wonderful things about keeping Oscar at Willowbrook for a couple of years had been the opportunity to ride through the beautiful hardwood forests at the back of the property. We could ride all the way to the lake, where several of the more ad-venturous riders (with brave horses) would strip off their saddles on the beach, hop on the horses bareback and go for a swim. Oscar, of course, with his life-long fear of water, would never do more than dip his toes, and dodge delicately out of the way as a wave lapped up on shore.

The entrance to the trails from Willowbrook's laneway was protected by a sizeable boulder, placed there to discourage people from taking motorized vehicles into the bush. This was good, since it reduced your chances of meeting a noisy ATV or snow mobile while out for a hack, but it also meant you had to ride your horse past that boulder. Most horses were understandably leery of this boulder the first few times they saw it. A large rock would, in the wilderness, offer a good hiding-place for a predator which could pounce on an unsuspecting horse if it wandered within range. After a few trips past this boulder, though, (with lots of cajoling, pleading, reassuring pats, help from more experienced horses etc.) most of the equines came to realize that there were, in fact, no cougars hiding behind this particular rock (or, indeed, any other rocks in our part of the world), and would pass the obstacle without giving it much more than a cursory glance. But some horses never got over it. Others, like my yellow-bellied Oscar, would suck up their courage to pass it without any trouble most days, but positively refuse to venture past without a fight on others. Same rock. Totally different response.

Far from the orderly, predictable world of physics that governs things like motorcycles, then, you are firmly in the realm of psychology in dealing with a horse, and not human psychology, either. Thinking like a human, difficult though it may be for most *homo sapiens* to accept, will get you precisely *nowhere* with a horse. They are not humans, for a start, and they are not predators as we are (or once were), but prey.

This is a huge distinction. Our thought-patterns are suited to pursuit and capture. While most of us no longer have to stalk and kill our own food, millions of years have hard-wired our brains to think as though we do, and these evolutionary patterns do not change overnight. We still show this hunting behaviour in our individualistic, competitive, goal-oriented, linear thinking. We are happiest when we have a clear goal and a predictable path to attaining it. We may work with others when necessary, but tend to be suspicious of their intentions and abilities. Team-work is an acquired art for most of us, not a natural instinct. I know. I teach college. Students universally detest group-work. It causes more stress and grief than final exams. Humans will co-operate if they must, but prefer individual glory (at least in the Western cultures). We admire self-reliance. We read books about self-help. We want to be self-starters. Self-made. We admire Dirty Harry, Rambo, Darwin, Einstein, The Lone Ranger, the cowboy, the lone wolf who takes on the system and wins.

The lone horse, on the other, hand is a dead horse. At least that's what evolution has conditioned him to believe. If you watch the Discovery Channel or Animal Planet, you will know that the first thing the lion, tiger or other predator tries to do is to separate its victim from the herd. "Alone" tends to equal "dead."

My beautiful Oscar knows this better than most. Make the mistake of bringing him into the barn alone, and you will soon have a sweating, screaming freak on your hands. He will pace his stall, whinny incessantly, rear, fret, worry and scream some more until someone does something about it (like smack herself in the head for forgetting, and go out to the paddock to fetch him a friend). Try to use tough love and leave him to wait it out and you may very well end up with colicky horse in need of the vet.

Not all horses are as bad as Oscar. Most can be conditioned to accept being alone, especially if they are in a safe, familiar environment, or with their human herd-mate. Even Oscar calms down once he's working, with a rider firmly in control (and presumably watching out for predators). But Oscar was 12 by the time I bought him, set in his ways, his natural fear of being alone made much, much worse by his previous owner who kept him alone, without the company of so much as a goat or donkey, for two years. Once reunited with horse companions, the idea of losing them again must have sent him into spasms of terror.

Horses are herd animals and have a pecking-order, rules and rituals. Herd members communicate in specific ways (the "get-out-of-my-space" pinned ears, the "you're my best friend" mutual grooming ritual, the "I'm top horse and get to eat first" nip on the rear end, and many, many more). While some of these messages are clear and easy for even a mere human to understand, others are much more subtle. Understanding what your horse is "saying" will certainly help your riding.

But there is more to being a prey animal than living in a herd. Even if you're with your friends, your odds of becoming some other animal's dinner are quite good if you do not hear the mountain lion coming, or don't start to run until the wolves have you surrounded. It's no accident or evil trick of nature that horses are jumpy and skittish, with a tendency to bolt at the slightest provocation. As far as they know, their lives depend on it. And while patient training can minimize these primitive responses, they will never entirely disappear. You can convince your horse that you are a trustworthy leader so he will follow you (jump an obstacle when you ask him to, for instance, without worrying what's on the other side), but you cannot change his nature. Even the best-trained, been-there-done-that horses will have an occasional melt-down. So if he spooks at that big boulder he walked past yesterday, it could be because the wind is rustling the leaves behind him on the trail today. Could that be a big cat, crouching, coiling up its body, ready to spring? "Hey, Human, can't you *hear* that? Let's get out of here!"

Challenging though the mental side of riding is, it's not the only thing you have to master. There is the whole physical element, too (and if anyone tries to tell you that riding – real riding, not being a passenger – is not physically difficult, tell them to try keeping their upper body perfectly still and balanced while sitting on a moving object and applying a different intensity of aid with each hand and leg while also putting pressure on one seat bone or the other or both and staying *relaxed* while they do it).

I have seen riders brought to tears by the sheer frustration of not being able – physically – to do what they need to do to accomplish something. I have been there myself!

"Make sure he's straight," my riding coach Karla would dictate (oh, that straightness thing again!), "and get him moving forward. Drive him with your seat" (ok, that means sitting deep in the saddle and pushing with my butt... but how exactly do I do that while I'm posting?). "Use your outside rein to keep his shoulder from popping out" (ok, so I keep a nice contact) "and get some flexion to the inside" (ok, little half-halts on the inside rein ought to do the trick) " but don't over-flex him!" (oh, sorry). "Now keep your inside leg on the girth with a little pressure" (right, I can do that) "but DON'T GET TENSE! RELAX!" (what?), "press down into the saddle with your inside seat bone" (you mean they move independently?) "but DON'T COLLAPSE YOUR HIP!" (collapse my hip? What the hell does that mean? And wasn't I just using my butt to drive?). "Now, slide your outside leg back slightly and squeeze. When he's lifting his outside hind leg" (and exactly when would THAT be?). "Keep your shoulders straight and you upper body still" (sure, and while I have nothing else to do up here, would you like me to balance your cheque book or compose a Sonata?).

So if you can manage to move every body part you own independently of every other, exert pressure with your legs while remaining perfectly relaxed, keep your body still while following your horse's motion, understand when he's moving each of his four feet and time your aids precisely to them, then you can begin to consider yourself something of a rider. Of course to a rider like Karla, it all seems perfectly simple. Some days she reminds me of a math teacher I had in high school who probably should have been working for NASA instead, and who would practically be crawling out of his skin after the first half hour of trying to make our dull little brains grasp what was, to him, the most elementary of concepts. Like Mr. Lennox, Karla saw no great difficulty in what she was asking me to do. She could do it in her sleep.

Fortunately, I had been taught to ride by a master of the classical style – a former cavalry officer from Hungary who initially scared the daylights out of us, his little teenage pupils, with his brusque style and the thick accent which made it hard to understand him and so to execute his commands as quickly as he expected. Once I got over the initial fear, though, I learned volumes from this accomplished horseman. That meant I got the basics right. I knew about training a horse to ride on contact instead of slapping a martingale on him to force it. I knew about impulsion and not over-relying on the reins to get things done, about using my weight and my seat and my legs correctly. And I could sit most of the fun stuff that a horse could throw at me. That cannot be said of all riders. I have found that many of the riders who look quite lovely on a horse, have no sticking-power whatsoever. Their horses can throw them with impunity, and many of them will. Repeatedly.

But there are others I have met who are masters of sitting -- and eventually calming -- a frightened horse. Often, it's pure self-preservation. They have to learn if they want to go on living. Yvonne was one such rider at Willowbrook. Her beautiful Trakhener mare was a lovely ride most of the time, could jump the moon, and had a perfectly charming disposition. But she was terrified of deer – of which there were quite a few in the woods at Willowbrook. Poor Vogue must have had a terrible experience with something fast and brown in her previous life, because at the sight of a deer she became virtually catatonic: she would plant her feet, raise her head, and tremble like she was having a seizure. Nothing her rider could do would distract or comfort her. She would stare at the deer, every muscle in her body wound tight, while Yvonne could do nothing but sit, waiting for the explosion that was bound to come. Without warning, Vogue would suddenly snap out of her mesmerized state, spin on her hocks and fly in the opposite direction. She never lost Yvonne once.

Seeing horses come flying out of the woods was not all that uncommon at Willowbrook. Sometimes their riders would have some semblance of control – Diana flew by me once, shouting: "I have no brakes!" but at least she had her steering and her sense of humour – while at other times the horse was clearly in charge. Occasionally, the horse was on its own, no rider in sight. That's when your stomach would do a sick little flip as you rushed towards the woods on your own horse (or the farm golf cart, if you didn't happen to be riding) your mind flipping through all the possible scenarios of what that horse could have done with his owner. But invariably the rider would come sprinting out of the woods too, a little worse for wear but running at top speed and worried about only one thing:

"Is _____ (insert horse's name) OK? Did she come back to the barn?"

I once tried to add some humour to the proceedings, following the "Yes, she's fine," with "Anna's taken her around back for a beating," but realized immediately that the rider was not amused. "No, no! I'm kidding!" I had to practically grab her by the arm. "It's a joke." But apparently not very funny.

There were lots of stories from those Willowbrook woods, but my favourite was Karla's "man-with-loonie-Lab" story.

Karla was training a particularly large Hanoverian for a client. Shaq was only three years old but stood a solid 18 hands tall, with lots of breadth and bone to support that height, too. There was nothing gangly about this beast, even at this young age. His feet were like dinner plates and his head the length of an average person's body. Karla was 5'4" and weighed maybe 110 pounds. It was an unequal match. Shaq didn't stand a chance.

He was a sweet horse, though, and learned quickly. His training was coming along very well, and one lovely autumn afternoon Karla decided to reward him for his hard work in the school ring by taking him for a hack. Since this was his first time out hacking, she did not go far, staying in the hayfield directly behind the barn. She was just rounding the far corner along the tree-line when a young Labrador Retriever burst out of the undergrowth directly in front of Karla and the astonished Shaq. Dog and horse both froze and looked at each other for a moment. Then the dog leapt into the air, landed, bowed with his belly close to the ground in the classic "let's play" position, and began to bark. With each "woof" he bounced several inches off the ground, spit flying, ears flapping in the air.

Shaq began to dance sideways and backwards away from the crazy beast, but the dog kept coming. Naturally, this concerned the horse. It was one thing to have this wild creature yipping at him from a distance, but when it began to close the gap between them, Shaq began to lose his cool.

"Call him off!" Karla yelled to the dog's owner who had finally caught up with his yipping charge.

"Scotch, come!" the young man ordered his dog.

Scotch (Scotch? What kind of name is Scotch?) ignored him.

"Come, Scotch. Off. Stop. Heel."

Nothing. The more the guy yelled, the more frantic the dog seemed to become. Did he think his owner was joining in the game of trying to scare this large creature out of its wits? Or did he think that the guy should maybe shoot the horse and rider so he, like a good gun dog, could retrieve them for him? Was he thinking anything at all?

Karla tried to turn Shaq and ride away from the dog, but Scotch chased after them, nipping at Shaq's heels. Perhaps a good kick from one of Shaq's massive hooves might have cured the dog of his obnoxious behaviour, but Shaq was not the kicking type. Afraid he'd get bitten, Karla turned him to face the dog again, and saw to her exasperation that the owner was doing nothing to help.

"Can you PLEASE get hold of this dog," she yelled.

"Well can you get your horse to stand still?" the guy yelled back. "He's getting the dog all excited!"

I have never heard Karla swear, but she assures me she swore this time. She backed Shaq up. Far. Reluctant to turn her back on the dog again. And suddenly the dog quit barking. It seemed he had decided the horse was no longer in his space. His hapless owner was able to sneak up from behind and grab him by the collar. Karla turned and rode away, deciding to "get" while the "getting was good," turning back only once.

"And get off our property!" she yelled at the dog-owner. Apparently he looked indignant.

But the ultimate example of horsemanship and grace under

pressure comes from an old riding instructor of Anna's. This particular gentleman had been riding all his life and was well into his seventies by the time Anna came to board and train at his barn. She was schooling her horse in the outdoor ring one day when Ben came out on a young green horse he was training. As soon as Ben mounted up, the young horse began to buck. Not one or two playful bucks or a few crow-hops to get the beans out of his system – no, a full-fledged bucking-bronco series of rodeo-worthy head-down, four-feet-in-the-air flips and twists and spins. Up and down and sideways he went, snorting and farting and shaking the ground as he bucked his way around the sand ring. And the old man rode it out, following the horse's erratic movements without apparent effort, foiling the horse's attempts to shake him. Sitting back, reins loose, calm, relaxed, amused, Ben sat the rodeo performance. Around and around they spun and whirled until the horse began to tire. Unable to dislodge his rider and losing his enthusiasm for the fight he eventually stopped, breathing hard.

The old man gathered up his reins, clucked gently, and rode around the ring a couple of times, looking intently at the ground. When he pulled up beside Anna, she noticed he looked a little funny.

"Have you seen my teeth?" he asked her. His dentures had flown out of his mouth during the proceedings. Anna nearly fell off her horse. "Can you help me find my teeth?"

But if we have trouble understanding our horses sometimes, they seem to have no such problems. A horse can tell the moment you're in his vicinity, what kind of day you've had and the mood you're bringing with you to the saddle. Not just that, but the same horse who will challenge you with a buck or playful spook just for the fun of it will become a patient babysitter when you put a beginner on his back.

I see this all the time with our special-needs riders. A horse will stop if he feels his rider slip off-balance, tolerate heels digging into his ribs, stand stock-still while his rider deals with an anxiety attack or seizure. The same horse, who responds with a flat-out gallop if an accomplished rider puts his leg on, will quietly ignore the aid to GO! if it's applied accidentally by a rider whose tight muscles or rattled nerves cause his legs to dig in.

It's a humbling thing to watch. If you're a rider who subscribes to the philosophy that we humans can always outsmart a horse; if you believe in getting your own way RIGHT NOW and just because you say so; if you always insist on having your horse move at your speed and never tune in and move at his, you may be missing the most meaningful part of being with horses. Our riders, who come with no agenda other than to spend some time with a horse, get it. Most days, I'm beginning to get it, too.

13

Life without horses is possible but pointless.
(Unknown)

As an English Lit major at university, I loved studying the classics. My favourites were the myths and plays of ancient Greece. All those gods. A god for every purpose. Along with gods of sun and earth and moon, of oceans and the underworld, of wisdom and healing, of love and war, there were gods of wine and thieves and making merry. And while they were immortal and divine, they also fell prey to emotions that we could identify as human. They turned damsels into trees out of jealousy, and themselves into swans and horses to secretly make love to women who had caught their eye; they started vicious wars over the favours of a mortal man, and devised hideous ways to keep their grip on power (like swallowing their own children, or locking their parents underground for eternity).

Still, they had their rules – for each other, and for the mortals they ruled from Mount Olympus. One of those rules had to do with any human (or god) getting too big for his (or her) britches. It's *hubris*, the undoing of all those great heroes of Greek tragedy, from Ajax spurning the offer of help from Athena to Oedipus thinking he could outsmart fate. Just when they thought they'd gotten away with it, BLAM. Down they'd go. Even the gods themselves could be blasted for their insolence if they tried to trick Zeus, the supreme ruler. And the Greek gods didn't just kill you quickly and get it over with. No, usually they would let you stew in your own juices. Masters of cruel and unusual punishment, they would force Sisyphus to push that rock up the hill only to have it roll back down as soon as he was done, time and time again for all eternity, or have an eagle eat Prometheus' liver every day as he stood chained to a desolate mountainside.

So I should have known better than to start getting smug, but I became cocky at some point. My careful management of my horses was paying off: they were sleek and shiny, glowing with health and apparently very content. We had managed to move them in once the barn was finished and gradually introduce them to big pastures, knee-high in grass.

"No more than an hour a day turn-out!" Ed had warned me when I'd asked for guidance on getting my hay-all-year-round herd adjusted to life with grassy pasture. "Then double it the next week, double again the week after that and so on, until you're back on a regular schedule."

"An hour a day?" I'd whined. "They'll lose their minds, cooped up for 23 hours every day.

"Do you have a place to let them stretch their legs?" Ed asked. "The arena, maybe?"

"Not unless you consider unfinished footing and piles of building material a suitable environment," I said glumly.

But much to my surprise the horses survived, minds relatively unaffected by too much confinement in their stalls, and didn't even give me a hard time about coming in when their hour of freedom was over. Thankfully, by the time we had actually moved them in, it was August and the grass was no longer lush and treacherous. The danger of colic being induced by too much grazing on rich forage had been dramatically reduced, and I was able to get the horses back onto a regular turn-out schedule in less than a month. They were very happy to wander their big, rolling fields, enjoying the grass beneath their feet and the warm sunshine on their backs.

By our second summer on the farm, the pastures had been mown down considerably. Now they looked like normal horse pastures instead of the overgrown hayfields they had been when we'd moved in. The barn and arena were working well, and although the house still needed lots of finishing touches, it wasn't anything we couldn't live with. I had also started up my therapeutic riding program, and a steady stream of clients was arriving at the barn door every week. By year three, I was having to juggle riders, volunteers and horses to try to fit everyone in. Word had spread about our program, and several people were driving an hour or more to bring their children riding. Our volunteers were devoted and hard-working, our horses steady, reliable, and enjoying their work. There were never enough hours in a day to get things done, but I could go to bed every night feeling good about what we had been able to accomplish.

And then Zeus threw his thunderbolt.

I was getting ready for a Friday-night lesson, grooming horses and chatting with Virginia, Stephanie, Edna and Krystal who were there to help out. Christopher and Michael were bringing horses from the big pasture to the paddock for the night, when I saw Rosie go down and roll almost as soon as she was through the gate. While this was not completely unusual, it was not normal behaviour for her, either, so I glanced out the window again in a few minutes. She was rolling again. When she stood up, she did not give that whole-body shake that usually follows a good roll on the ground, starting at the nose and progressing right down to the tail: that satisfied, "wow that felt good" sort of finish to a nice scratch. Instead, she simply stood, head down, beside Ronan.

By this time I was headed out to the paddock with a lead rope in my hand, and when she went down again before I got to her, I knew she was in trouble. I clipped the rope to her halter and led her into the arena, grabbing the cordless phone on my way by. I was dialing the vet's number as we walked around. She tried dropping to the ground, but I was able to stop her. Once the call was completed and the vet – finishing up a call supposedly not too far away – soon to be on his way, I focused on Rosie. She was strangely crouched down as she walked, looking several inches shorter than normal, and in obvious pain. But she was not sweating badly, nor was her breathing alarmingly fast. I allowed myself some hope.

It was mid-June and the arena was very warm. I decided to take Rosie to the outdoor sand ring, and continue our walk there. While I was more comfortable, it soon became obvious that Rosie was becoming less so. She was now quite determined to go down again and roll, and it took increasing amounts of pulling on the lead rope, shouting, and smacking her with the end of the lead shank to keep her on her feet. Virginia, Edna and the kids did their best to help me, encouraging Rosie to walk. Stephanie brought out a bucket of cool water and we sponged Rosie down, hoping to make her feel a little better.

Then she went down, and I could do nothing to stop her. I was able to keep her from rolling, though, and was happy about that. It's the rolling that's dangerous when a horse colics. As she tries to reduce the pain in her belly by thrashing on the ground, she may twist an intestine, and then it's deadly. If operated on quickly, the horse may be saved, but not always. As long as she stayed on her chest and belly I let her lie there while we both rested, then pulled her to her feet again. I asked one of the kids for the lungeing whip, and next time she tried to go down I went after her that much harder. She stayed on her feet, but only for a while. Half-way around the ring she threw herself down and this time she rolled. Once she was over, I managed to pin her down on her side. Virginia tried to come and hold her legs down, and it was all I could do to convince her to stand back. If Rosie flailed those feet as she tried to roll again or to get up, she could break Virginia's leg or crack her skull. A horse in pain can be a very dangerous thing.

But Rosie was not wild. She lay on her side for a while, then, with all of us yelling encouragement and me pulling on the lead rope, she heaved herself to her feet again. Time dragged on as I pulled that poor horse around the sand ring, the sound of a car approaching snapping my head to see if the vet was at long last coming, then disappointment when it was not him. My lesson showed up first – a wonderful young man named Nicholas who adored animals and music, spent most of each lesson telling Wilby what a good horse he was, and singing Rihanna songs. I sent Virginia to head him off. I did not want him to see Rosie suffering. She explained to his father what the situation was, and they left again. Still no vet.

When Ed finally did arrive, Rosie was down again, flat on her side, head in the sand, not moving. We tried to get her to her feet so Ed could do a rectal exam, but she would not get up. Even after the drugs kicked in to dull her pain, Rosie could not be convinced to get to her feet. She tried once, half-heartedly, but fell down again and flopped over. By this time I was crying, because I knew it was over. Ed examined her as best he could while she lay on the ground, but it was really a moot point. All you had to do was look at her eyes to know.

I asked Virginia to get everyone out of there. I did not want the kids to see what had to happen next, so they gathered up their things and headed home. While Ed got the drugs and IV ready, I asked the question I knew he could not answer. Why? What had happened? Why today? Why her? What was I doing wrong?

"If we knew what causes colic," Ed said, "we could get rid of colic. We know many of the things that do. We know what tends to bring it on. But to tell you what caused a particular colic in a particular horse on a given day is practically impossible. Sometimes there's something that turns up in a necropsy – a tumour or obstruction in the intestines, for example. But most often there is not. Sometimes there's an obvious change in the horse's life: a new barn, different feed, reaction to a drug. But most often there is not. All you can do is try to minimize the risks, but you can never prevent it completely. Not yet, anyway."

I don't know if that made me feel better or worse. I thought I had it figured out: the right amount of feed, exercise, turn-out. Lots of water always on hand. No drastic changes in anything in the horses' lives. Regular de-worming. You name it, I did it. And then this. I think I heard the gods on Olympus laughing.

There was no question of attempting the drive to Guelph. By the time Ed administered the euthanasia, Rosie was barely breathing.

I went into a deep funk after that. What was the point? I wondered. Just what was I accomplishing here? I'd seen my farm as some sort of sanctuary – a place where horses would be honoured and respected, and those people who otherwise would never be able to ride could come and interact with these wonderful creatures; benefit from all they had to give. But who was I kidding? I could not even keep them alive!

I pointed this out to Ed next time he was at the farm to vaccinate the horses, tears rolling down my face.

"Are you kidding," he chastised me. "Look at this place. It's gorgeous. Your horses are positively glowing with health."

"Yeah," I said, "except for the dead ones."

He pinned me with a hard look.

"You know," he said, "I tell people, if you're going to have livestock, you're going to have dead stock, too. If you can't deal with that, then stick to growing corn."

That made me laugh.

But the funk stuck hard. My ridiculously well-developed sense of optimism usually pulls me out of bluesy moods quickly, but not this time. I found it hard to motivate myself for lessons or riding, and did my chores in auto-pilot mode, my mind spinning around the various possibilities about what to do next. I seriously considered selling. Couldn't we just sell the farm and most of the horses? I could keep Henk and maybe Wilby, if I could afford to board them both, and we could go live in a nice condo in town. No animals. No land. The dogs could go back to their breeders, the cats could stay with the farm. I'd spend my time reading and going to the theatre instead of mucking stalls and teaching lessons. I'd have no responsibility for living creatures other than myself and whatever influence the kids still let me have in their lives. A boarding stable would look after the horses. It had a certain appeal. I even half-heartedly tried to track down a realtor who had some experience with horse farms.

I felt I'd broken some unspoken promise in letting Rosie die. Hadn't I bragged about giving her a second chance in life? Hadn't I verbally beaten up those people who had been responsible for her miserable early months and the slaughter-house she'd so narrowly escaped? But in the end they had not been the ones who'd killed her. I had. Whatever it was I'd done that I shouldn't have, or didn't do that needed to be done, she was dead now because of it, and I didn't even fully understand why. Was this my punishment for those feelings of superiority that snuck in when I told people about "rescuing" the three babies from their wretched existence?

Maybe. But while I was spending too much time wallowing in self-pity, the demands of the farm never let up. There were horses to feed, groom and ride. Stalls to muck. Dogs to look after. Lessons to teach. I couldn't just turn everything off and crawl into bed with a bucket of ice cream and old movies on TV. Besides, Greek drama was for gods and heroes in far-away exotic places. What made me think anyone on Mount Olympus had the slightest interest in what I said or did? Weren't they too busy with warriors and kings? Instead of some cosmic come-uppance, was this not, after all, just one of those things that happens, in spite of your best efforts to prevent it? When I'd decided, all those years ago, to bring my horses home and become a horsewoman in the full sense of the word, was this not part of the deal?

I lost a lot of sleep. I still see Rosie in my dreams. I have a plait of her tail-hair in my house along with her photo and the name-plate from her stall. I miss that mare.

Eventually the routines of daily life, not least of them the mind-less zen-like ritual of the pitchfork cleaning stalls, began to dissipate the blues. I taught fewer lessons for a month and rode more. My own therapy through riding, letting the quest to perfect that pesky shoulder-in replace the visions of a dying Rosie in my mind. Of course it worked. They don't call it therapeutic riding for nothing.

14

A man on a horse is spiritually as well
as physically bigger than a man on foot.
(John Steinbeck)

John Steinbeck? Let me begin by saying that John Steinbeck found several ingenious ways to scar my psyche with the power of his words. None was more devastating than his seemingly child-friendly little novella, *The Red Pony*. Of course, as it turns out, this is *not* a kid's book, so part of the fault lies with my father for giving it to me to read around the age of ten. Still, I place most of the blame on the writer. A couple of the scenes in that book will never leave me, not least because they are so well written that I can *see* the action in my mind. Still. Forty years later. The killing of the mare by smashing in her forehead, and the foal being dragged out of her slashed-open belly. Or the death of the red pony himself, and that damned buzzard landing on his head and plucking out his eyeball. I mean, what *is* that about? It's even worse than the death of Bambi's mother or the kid having to shoot his own dog in *Old Yeller*. It's worse because there's no cheap sentimentality about it and because Steinbeck fully understood the bond between horses and mankind. He used that understanding to twist the knife in the wound he'd made.

He knew just how spiritually big a horse could make you, and what it costs to lose him.

Because horses elevate you. You cannot seriously contemplate the greatness of a horse – his generosity of spirit, his kindness, his nobility – without becoming a little bit more noble yourself in the process.

Unlike dogs, who take us as their pack leaders and devote themselves to us unconditionally, or cats which tolerate our existence in their world because it brings them certain pleasures, horses willingly share with us the greatness of their power and spirit, without ever becoming servile. A horse well trained and correctly ridden loses nothing of his own self while making the human on his back incomparably greater. No other animal has done so much to lift the human species out of want and drudgery, and sometimes received so little in return.

We have used the horse's physical power to take control of the world around us so that we could dominate all that we saw. We have used his bravery to ride him into battle so that we could dominate our fellow human beings, too. We have taught the horse to run faster, jump higher, and leap into the air at our command for our own pleasure. We have eaten him. Abused him. Left him broken and maimed by our unreasonable demands. We have written him off as a quaint relic of the past. We have elevated him to the level of art. We have recognized – sometimes explicitly when we use them to heal the shattered spirits of broken soldiers and sometimes tacitly when we soothe our frazzled nerves with a quick visit to the barn – that horses have the power to make us whole again.

I am in awe, sometimes, as I look out my bedroom window and see the horses grazing in their paddock. How did we come to be blessed with this kind of beauty in our lives?

In my world, angels have four legs. Their feathers don't grow on wings sprouting from their backs, but rather around their ankles, like Hermes' wings – the wings he loaned to Perseus to help him slay the Gorgon Medusa. Like Hermes, messenger of the gods and helper to man, the horse has favoured mankind with his power. Whether carrying a warrior into battle or pulling the plow in a furrowed field, chasing game or teaching a child about freedom, the horse has written himself into our story and made us infinitely better for it.

My horses lend their strength and spirit to some twenty riders per week, forty-eight weeks per year. Some riders come for only a single session a year, some come for every one of those forty-eight weeks. Like Krystal, some return to volunteer their time. Having once discovered life with horses, they will not let it go again. No one leaves unchanged. Riders, parents, volunteers – we all are better for the time spent in the company of horses.